JACKSON & POWELL ON
PROFESSIONAL LIABILITY

VOLUMES IN THE COMMON LAW LIBRARY

JACKSON & POWELL ON PROFESSIONAL LIABILITY

FIRST SUPPLEMENT TO THE NINTH EDITION

Law stated as at 30 September 2022

SWEET & MAXWELL

THOMSON REUTERS

Published in 2023 by Thomson Reuters,
trading as Sweet & Maxwell. Thomson Reuters is registered in England &
Wales, Company No. 1679046.
Registered office and address for service: 5 Canada Square, Canary Wharf,
London E14 5AQ.

For further information on our products and services, visit *http://
www.sweetandmaxwell.co.uk.*

Computerset by Sweet & Maxwell.
Printed and bound by CPI Group (UK) Ltd, Croydon, CR0 4YY.
A CIP catalogue record of this book is available from the British Library.

Main Work ISBN (print): 978-0-414-09040-8

First supplement ISBN (print): 978-0-414-10434-1

First supplement ISBN (e-book): 978-0-414-10437-2

First supplement ISBN (print and e-book): 978-0-414-10435-8

FSC
www.fsc.org
MIX
Paper | Supporting
responsible forestry
FSC® C013604

PREFACE TO THE FIRST SUPPLEMENT OF THE NINTH EDITION

Ever since the third edition of *Jackson & Powell on Professional Negligence* was published in 1992, once a year the editors have sent to press a supplement to the main work, right up until the fifth year, whereupon a new edition has been prepared, to allow for changes in structure or content that reflect important developments in the field. To this end, this first supplement to the ninth edition is no different to any of the others prepared to accompany past editions, insofar as it documents the most significant developments in case law and legislation, alongside academic and practitioner commentary by leading experts. However, unlike any past edition or supplement, shortly after the publication of the ninth edition of *Jackson & Powell on Professional Liability* the team experienced the unexpected and major loss of one of its General Editors, Mark Cannon QC (1961–2022).

For over 35 years, Mark practised from 4 New Square as a widely recognised expert in commercial, construction, and insurance law, serving most recently as its Head of Chambers, from 2017 to 2021. Mark, who by the time of his untimely death had been a Bencher of the Middle Temple since 2014, joined chambers as a pupil in 1987, having been called to the Bar in 1985. Mark took silk in 2008 and, from 2009 to 2011, served as a highly regarded chairman of the Professional Negligence Bar Association.

Among Mark's many contributions to legal literature,[1] in 1992 Mark joined Sir Rupert Jackson and John Powell QC as one of only five editors of what was then the newly titled *Jackson & Powell on Professional Negligence*.[2] From his appointment to the third edition as an editor, through to his role as General Editor of the eighth edition,[3] *Jackson & Powell* has benefited hugely from Mark's incisive and timely contributions over the course of his thirty-year editorial tenure, during which time he played an instrumental role in overseeing a shift in the work's focus, along with its later renaming to *Jackson & Powell on Professional Liability*. He was at the very heart of this work. He was also an extremely generous and kind friend and colleague and will be sorely missed by many at Chambers and beyond.

As with the main work, the general editors retain overall responsibility for the supplement and the law is stated as at 30 September 2022. We are, as ever, grateful to our publishers, Sweet & Maxwell, and particularly to Sohini Banerjee and

---

[1] Alongside his work as an editor and General Editor of *Jackson & Powell on Professional Liability*, Mark collaborated with Brendan McGurk of Monckton Chambers to produce the leading monograph *Professional Liability Insurance*, 1st edn (Oxford: Oxford University Press, 2010). A second edition of the work was published in 2016.

[2] R. M. Jackson, J. L. Powell and others (eds), *Jackson & Powell on Professional Negligence*, 3rd edn (London: Sweet & Maxwell, 1992), v. See too, "A Brief History" from p.vii of the ninth edition published in 2022.

[3] Mark began acting as lead General Editor of *Jackson & Powell on Professional Liability*, alongside Hugh Evans and Roger Stewart KC, from the first supplement of the eighth edition, published in 2018.

Michelle Afford for their kindness and assistance in our preparation of this supplement.

The General Editors, Academic Editor, and Editors
Jackson & Powell on Professional Liability

4 New Square,
Lincoln's Inn,
London WC2A 3RJ

30 September 2022

HOW TO USE THIS SUPPLEMENT

This is the First Supplement to the Ninth Edition of *Jackson & Powell on Professional Liability* and has been compiled according to the structure of the main volume.

At the beginning of each chapter of this Supplement, a mini table of contents of the sections in the main volume has been included. Where a heading in this table of contents has been marked by the symbol ■ there is relevant information in this Supplement to which you should refer.

Within each chapter, updating information is referenced to the relevant paragraph in the main volume.

TABLE OF CONTENTS

TABLE OF CASES

TABLE OF STATUTES

All references are to paragraph numbers.

TABLE OF STATUTORY INSTRUMENTS

All references are to paragraph numbers.

CHAPTER 1

THE NATURE OF PROFESSIONAL LIABILITY AND THE PROFESSIONS

TABLE OF CONTENTS

1. PROFESSIONAL LIABILITY AND THE PROFESSIONS

Replace paragraph 1-001 (to incorporate footnote updates) with:

As noted in recent editions of this book, "professional liability" defines a wider realm of causes of action than "professional negligence". The latter term invites association with the tort of negligence. Contract rather than tort, however, provides the framework for resolving the vast majority of claims against members of professions.[1] Analysis follows the conventional course of first ascertaining the nature of the bargain as reflected in express and implied terms.[2] Tort needs to be considered only to the extent necessary to overcome perceived obstacles arising from the contractual analysis. Statutory liabilities may also be incurred under various statutes (such as for defective service under the Consumer Rights Act 2015). Further, fiduciary duties are conceptually distinct from duties of care,[3] which underpin claims for professional liability based on contract and tort.[4] Nevertheless, such duties not only are highly pertinent to a text spanning the liability of lawyers, medical practitioners, accountants, and financial practitioners, but also provide important context for claims based on contract, tort and statute.[5]

1-001

[1] H.G. Beale and others (eds), *Chitty on Contracts*, 34th edn (London: Sweet & Maxwell, 2021), Vol.2; J. Gould and others, *The Law of Legal Services and Practice*, 2nd edn (London: LexisNexis, 2019), Ch.7 and S. Salzedo and T. Singla, *Accountants' Negligence and Liability*, 2nd edn (London: Bloomsbury Professional, 2021), Ch.1 at 1.10 and following, cf. R. Mulheron, "Duties in Contract and Tort" in J. Laing, J. McHale, Sir Ian Kennedy, A. Grubb and others (eds), *Principles of Medical Law*, 4th edn (Oxford: Oxford University Press, 2017), Ch.3.

[2] Beale and others (eds), *Chitty on Contracts*, 34th edn, Vol.1, see too, E. McKendrick "Contract" in A.S. Burrows (Lord Burrows) (ed.), *English Private Law*, 3rd edn (Oxford: Oxford University Press, 2013), Ch.8.

[3] Dame Sarah Worthington, *Equity*, 2nd edn (Oxford: Oxford University Press, 2006), Ch.5, 129 and following; P.B. Miller and A.S. Gold (eds), *Contract, Status and Fiduciary Law* (Oxford: Oxford University Press, 2016), Pts 1 and 2; J. Glister and J. Lee (eds), *Hanbury & Martin Modern Equity*, 22nd edn (London: Sweet & Maxwell, 2021), Ch.22 and M.A. Jones, A. Dugdale and others (eds), *Clerk & Lindsell on Torts*, 23rd edn (London: Sweet & Maxwell, 2020, 2nd supp, 2022), Chs 1 and 2.

[4] ibid., see too fn.1, and R. Singh (Singh LJ) "Foreword" in K. Hamer, *Professional Conduct Casebook*, 3rd edn (Oxford: Oxford University Press, 2019), p.v.

[5] See, for example, I. Miller and others (eds), *Cordery on Legal Services*, 9th edn, Issue 129 (London: LexisNexis, 2022); J. Kirk, R. Kingham and others (eds), *Encyclopedia of Financial Services Law*, Rel.130 (London: Sweet & Maxwell, 2022), Pt 1, Introduction; S. Salzedo and T. Singla, *Accountants' Negligence and Liability*, 2nd edn (London: Bloomsbury Professional, 2021), and J. Laing and others (eds), *Principles of Medical Law*, 4th edn (Oxford: Oxford University Press, 2017). See too, M. Davies, *Solicitors' Negligence and Liability* (Oxford: Oxford University Press, 2008), p.vi.

Replace footnote 8 with:

1-002   [8] D. Greenberg (ed.) *Stroud's Judicial Dictionary of Words and Phrases*, 10th edn (London: Sweet & Maxwell, 2020, 2nd supp, 2022) and M. Dent and others, "The Changing World of Professions and Professionalism" in M. Dent, I.L. Bourgeault, J-L. Denis, and E. Kuhlmann (eds), *The Routledge Companion to the Professions and Professionalism* (Oxford: Routledge, 2016), 1. See too, R. Abel, "Lawyers and Legal Services" in P. Cane and M. Tushnet (eds), *The Oxford Handbook of Legal Studies* (Oxford: Oxford University Press, 2003), Pt VI, Ch.35, for example.

Replace list in paragraph 1-003 (to incorporate changes to footnotes 10 and 13) with:

1-003   1.   *The nature of the work.* The work done is skilled and specialised. A substantial part of the work is mental rather than manual. A period of theoretical and practical training is usually required before the work can be adequately performed. It often takes place in a regulated environment (e.g. a firm or hospital), and is usually subject to specific rules about the kind of practise one may carry on. These rules arise from, and are justified by, the need to protect the public interest in the work being performed competently and in way which does not unduly restrict competition.

2.   *The moral aspect.* Practitioners are usually committed, or are expected to be committed, to certain moral principles, which go beyond the general duty of honesty.[10] They are expected to provide a high standard of service for its own sake. They are expected to be particularly concerned about the duty of confidentiality. They also, normally, owe a wider duty to the community, which may on occasions transcend the duty to a particular client or patient.[11]

3.   *Collective organisation.* Practitioners usually belong to a professional body which oversees admission and seeks to uphold commonly agreed standards of the profession. Such bodies normally set the educational and examination requirements of prospective registrants, and the revalidation of existing practitioners. Such bodies therefore usually issue codes pertaining to professional conduct and ethics.[12]

4.   *Status.* Most professions have a high status in the community, and thereby attract widespread public trust.[13] Some of their privileges are conferred by Parliament, while others are granted by common consent.

[10] A. Boon, *Lawyers' Ethics and Professional Responsibility* (Oxford: Hart Publishing, 2015), Ch.1, 30 and following; S. Salzedo and T. Singla, *Accountants' Negligence and Liability*, 2nd edn (London: Bloomsbury Professional, 2021), Ch.1; and D. Gomez and others (eds), *The Regulation of Healthcare Professionals: Law, Principle and Process*, 2nd edn (London: Sweet & Maxwell, 2019), Ch.30, para.30-077 especially. More broadly, see R.H. Tawney, *The Acquisitive Society* (Brighton: Harvester Press, 1982) and T.J. Johnson, *Professions and Power* (Oxford: Routledge, 2017, reprint, first published in 1972), and fnn. 6, 7, and 8 on the professions.

[11] For example, a doctor's duty to prevent the spread of contagious diseases may outweigh his duty to a particular patient. An accountant, certifying the accounts of a firm of solicitors or auditing the accounts of a public company, may find himself obliged to act contrary to the immediate interests of his clients. Similarly, a barrister or solicitor is under a professional obligation to draw the court's attention to relevant authorities, even if they are adverse to his client's case. And, architects have a responsibility for public safety and environmental considerations, which go beyond their immediate duty to the client. Thus, the public responsibility assumed by a professional far exceeds that which is expected of

the average person: see, for example, A. Boon, *Lawyers' Ethics and Professional Responsibility* (Oxford: Hart Publishing, 2015), Ch.1, 30 and following, on law.

[12] The late sociologist Ralf Dahrendorf argued that the crucial distinction between professions in Britain and those on the European continent is that, in Britain, the professions are self-governing and independent, whereas most in Europe are regulated by the state. In "Defence of the English Professions" (1984) *Journal of the Royal Society of Medicine*, Vol.77, 178, Dahrendorf points out that if any major profession is slack in the enforcement of its own standards, public confidence in all professions is undermined: see here M. Davies, "The Demise of Professional Self-Regulation? Evidence from the Ideal Professions of Medicine and Law" (2010) P.N. Vol.26, 3-38; D. Gomez and others (eds), *The Regulation of Healthcare Professionals: Law, Principle and Process*, 2nd edn (London: Sweet & Maxwell, 2019), Ch.1, s.2; A. Boon, *Lawyers' Ethics and Professional Responsibility* (Oxford: Hart Publishing, 2015), Ch.3, 64 and following and D. Fairgreive and D. Squires, *The Negligence and Liability of Public Authorities*, 2nd edn (Oxford: Oxford University Press, 2019), Ch.14, s.E. paras 14.58 and following.

[13] As Lord Bingham notably observed in *Bolton v The Law Society*, the overriding aim of a professional body should be to regulate in such a way as to ensure "... every member, of whatever standing, may be trusted to the ends of the earth" by a client or patient: [1993] EWCA Civ 32 at 15; [1994] W.L.R. 512 at 518. However, major failings or scandals have had the effect of weaken public trust in some professions, regardless of the actual or perceived importance some may have in society, such as healthcare professionals, for example. Consequently, many professions have undergone major regulatory and disciplinary reform in recent decades, with a view to maintaining public confidence and increasing transparency: see here, for example, Gomez and others (eds), *The Regulation of Healthcare Professionals: Law, Principle and Process*, 2nd edn (London: Sweet & Maxwell, 2019), Ch.1, s.2 on healthcare, I. Miller and others (eds), *Cordery on Legal Services*, 9th edn, Issue 129 (London: LexisNexis, 2022), Div A, s.1 on law; J. Kirk, R. Kingham and others (eds), *Encyclopedia of Financial Services Law*, Rel.130 (London: Sweet & Maxwell, 2022), Pt 1 on financial services, and S. Salzedo and T. Singla, *Accountants' Negligence and Liability*, 2nd edn (London: Bloomsbury Professional, 2021), Ch.14, 479 on accountancy.

Replace footnote 14 with:

[14] Judicial discussion about the nature of professions occurs principally in tax cases, see *IRC v Maxse* [1919] 1 K.B. 647 at 657 per Scrutton LJ; *Currie v IRC* [1921] 2 K.B. 332 at 343 per Scrutton LJ; *Carr v IRC* [1944] 2 All E.R. 163 at 166–167 per Du Parcq LJ. See too, fn 6, 7 and 8, especially A. Boon, *The Conduct and Ethics of Lawyers in England and Wales*, 3rd edn (Oxford: Hart Publishing, 2015) and R. Abel, "Lawyers and Legal Services" in P. Cane and M. Tushnet (eds), *The Oxford Handbook of Legal Studies* (Oxford: Oxford University Press, 2003), Pt VI, Ch.35. See too, B. Lange "Regulation" in P. Cane and J. Conaghan, *The New Oxford Companion to Law* (Oxford: Oxford University Press, 2008), 996.

1-007

2. RISK TRANSFERRED AND RISK RETAINED

Replace footnote 18 with:

[18] As members of the judiciary, Kenneth Hamer, and others have observed, an ever-increasing number of "significant" cases continue to come before the higher courts: see Singh LJ, "Foreword", and K. Hamer "Preface", K. Hamer, *Professional Conduct Casebook*, 3rd edn (Oxford: Oxford University Press, 2019), pp.v and vii respectively, and Lord Lloyd Jones, "Foreword" in K. Hamer, *Professional Conduct Casebook*, 2nd edn (Oxford: Oxford University Press, 2015), p.v. See too, Lord Hoffmann, "Preface" in S. Salzedo and T. Singla, *Accountants' Negligence and Liability*, 2nd edn (London: Bloomsbury Professional, 2021), p.vii.

1-009

CHAPTER 2

DUTIES AND OBLIGATIONS

TABLE OF CONTENTS

1. PROFESSIONAL LIABILITY

(b) The Paradigm: Clients and Express Contracts

Replace heading footnote 3 with:

The SAAMCO scope of duty question[3]

2-005

[3] A reference to Lord Hoffmann's speech in *South Australia Asset Management Corp v York Montague Ltd* [1997] A.C. 191. *SAAMCO* has been the subject of consideration by the Supreme Court on two more recent occasions: in *Hughes-Holland v BPE Solicitors* [2017] UKSC 21; [2018] A.C. 599; and in the

linked appeals in *Manchester Building Society v Grant Thornton UK LLP* [2021] UKSC 20; [2022] A.C. 783 and *Khan v Meadows* [2021] UKSC 21; [2022] A.C. 852.

Replace paragraph 2-005 (to incorporate footnote updates) with:

Secondly, even assuming A owes B a contractual obligation to carry out a particular task, B must demonstrate that A's obligation extends to protecting B from the risks of harm that have eventuated (and led to B's loss).[4] This is commonly known as the *SAAMCO* scope of duty question, albeit it has recently been relabelled by the Supreme Court.[5]

[4] See paras 2-143 to 2-171. In the recent case of *Spire Property Development LLP v Withers LLP* [2022] EWCA Civ 970; [2022] P.N.L.R. 27, the Court of Appeal confirmed that an analysis of the extent of the professional's obligation precedes, and is separate from, an analysis of the scope of that obligation for the purposes of *SAAMCO*—see Carr LJ at [70]–[71].

[5] *Manchester Building Society v Grant Thornton UK LLP* [2021] UKSC 20; [2022] A.C. 783 and *Khan v Meadows* [2021] UKSC 21; [2022] A.C. 852.

(c)   Non-Clients: Contractual and Tortious Claims

Other matters

Replace list item "2." (to incorporate footnote 17 update) with:

2.   *The SAAMCO scope of duty enquiry* Which of B's losses (if any) fall within   **2-010**
the scope of the obligation or duty A owes to B?[17]

[17] This is the same issue as described at para.2-005. See paras 2-143 to 2-171. In the recent case of *Spire Property Development LLP v Withers LLP* [2022] EWCA Civ 970; [2022] P.N.L.R. 27, the Court of Appeal confirmed that an analysis of the extent of the professional's implied obligation and/or duty precedes, and is separate from, an analysis of the scope of that obligation/duty for the purposes of *SAAMCO*—see Carr LJ at [70]–[71].

(e)   Regulation and Professional Standards

Replace footnote 24 with:

[24] See I. Miller and others (eds), *Cordery on Legal Services*, 9th edn, Issue 129 (London: LexisNexis,   **2-015**
2022), Div. F, sections 3B and 3C; G. Treverton-Jones and J. Potts, "The Decision to Prosecute" in Dame Alison Foster, G. Treverton-Jones, and S. Hanif (eds), *Disciplinary and Regulatory Proceedings*, 10th edn (London: LexisNexis, 2019), Ch.6 for discussion.

It has been held, for example, that the anti-money laundering regime, applicable to solicitors as part of their regulatory code, does not give rise to a civilly actionable duty on the part of the solicitors to carry out identity checks on their own client—see *P&P Property Ltd v Owen White & Catlin LLP* [2018] EWCA Civ 1082; [2019] Ch. 273 at [78] per Patten LJ and *Lennon v Englefield* [2021] EWHC 1473 (QB); [2022] P.N.L.R. 3 at [82] per HHJ Gosnell (sitting as a Judge of the High Court).

Replace footnote 27 with:

[27] See M. A. Jones, A. Dugdale and others (eds), *Clerk & Lindsell on Torts*, 23rd edn (London: Sweet   **2-016**
& Maxwell, 2020, 2nd supp, 2022), Ch.8.

(f)   Other bases of professional liability

Deceit

Replace footnote 37 with:

[37] [2018] EWHC 2877 (Ch). For a detailed review of the tort of deceit, see *Clerk & Lindsell on Torts*   **2-022**
(2020, 2nd supp 2022), Ch.17.

Tort of conspiracy

Replace footnote 41 with:

2-025   41 For a more detailed analysis of tortious claims for conspiracy, see *Clerk & Lindsell on Torts* (2020, 2nd supp 2022), Ch.23, Section 5. A claim in conspiracy (and on other bases) against a solicitor failed in *De Krassel v Chu Vincent* [2010] 2 H.K.L.R.D. 937.

2.   CONTRACTUAL OBLIGATIONS

(a)   The Position at Common Law

(i)   *Contracts of engagement*

Introduction

Replace footnote 45 with:

2-027   45 The most obvious exception here may be medical patients, such as those in receipt of services from the National Health Service, unless such a provision is privately commissioned. Professor Shaun Pattinson observes: "Private patients will enter in to a contractual relationship by paying for the service (directly or by insurance), whereas the relationship between an NHS doctor and patient is based upon a statutory obligation rather than contract," see S. Pattinson, *Medical Law and Ethics*, 6th edn (London: Sweet and Maxwell, 2020), p.52 at para.3-002; see too *Reynolds v Health First Medical Group* [2000] Lloyd's Rep. Med. 240 and *Pfizer Corp v Ministry of Health* [1965] A.C. 512. Further, see R. Mulheron, "Duties in Contract and Tort" in J. Laing, J. McHale, Sir Ian Kennedy, A. Grubb and others (eds), *Principles of Medical Law*, 4th edn (Oxford: Oxford University Press, 2017), Ch.3. Of course, analogy is sometimes mistakenly drawn between NHS patients and clients of a barrister or solicitor in receipt of state funded representation, such as Legal Aid. However, like many professions, and in difference to healthcare, the services of solicitors and barristers (albeit to a much lesser degree) are perennially dependent on a contractual relation between practitioner and client: see H.G. Beale and others (eds), *Chitty on Contracts*, 34th edn (London: Sweet & Maxwell 2021), Vol.I, Ch.21, para.21-016 and J. Gould and others, *The Law of Legal Services and Practice*, 2nd edn (London: LexisNexis, 2019), Chs 7 and 12, for discussion. See too, Ch.11 (on solicitors), 12 (on barristers) and 13 (on medical practitioners).

Contractual limitations upon the extent of the engagement

Replace footnote 68 with:

2-037   68 See *Chitty on Contracts* (2021), para.15-012.

(ii)   *Other Express Contracts*

Certificates or warranty letters

Replace footnote 103 with:

2-049   103 See *Chitty on Contracts* (2021), Vol.I, Ch.6.

(iii)   *Implied Contracts*

The test for an implied contract

Replace footnote 106 with:

2-051   106 *NDH Properties Ltd v Lupton Fawcett LLP* [2020] EWHC 3056 (Ch); [2021] P.N.L.R. 8 at [82] per Snowden J, adopting the approach taken by Arnold J in *Caliendo v Mishcon de Reya* [2016] EWHC 150 (Ch) at [682] and by Hamblen J in *Brown v InnovatorOne Plc* [2012] EWHC 1321 (Comm) at [1016]. For a recent example, see *McDonnell v Dass Legal Solutions (MK) Law Ltd* [2022] EWHC 991 (QB); [2022] Costs L.R. 855 (no implied retainer in relation to a firm of solicitors).

(b) Statutory Intervention

(ii) The Consumer Rights Act 2015

The Consumer Rights Act 2015

Replace footnote 113 with:

[113] For a general commentary and introduction to consumer law and contracts, see *Chitty on Contracts* (2021), Vol.II, Ch.40; G. Hickinbottom (Hickinbottom LJ), S. Sime, D. French and others (eds), *Blackstone's Civil Practice 2022: The Commentary* (Oxford: Oxford University Press, 2022), Ch.89, 1767 and following, as relevant, and Sir Martin Moore-Bick, P.K.J. Thompson and others (eds), *The Civil Court Practice 2022* (London: LexisNexis, 2022, supp August 2022), Vol.2, 4497, as relevant.

2-057

4. TORTIOUS DUTIES

(a) The Tort of Negligence

Introduction

Replace footnote 139 with:

[139] For a general discussion of the tort of negligence, which is beyond the scope of this book, see M. Armitage and others, *Charlesworth & Percy on Negligence*, 15th edn (London: Sweet & Maxwell, 2022). See, too, J. Plunket, *Duty of Care in Negligence* (Oxford: Hart Publishing, 2019) and C. Mitchell and P. Mitchell (eds), *Landmark Cases in the Law of Tort* (Oxford: Hart Publishing, 2010).

2-066

The interlinked facets of the duty question

Replace footnote 143 with:

[143] See, respectively, [2021] UKSC 20; [2022] A.C. 783 and [2021] UKSC 21; [2022] A.C. 852. See, for a detailed analysis of these appeals, paras 2-157 to 2-165, when addressing the *SAAMCO* scope of duty question.

2-067

The approach taken in the next two sections of this chapter

Replace footnote 144 with:

[144] See, respectively, [2021] UKSC 20; [2022] A.C. 783 and [2021] UKSC 21; [2022] A.C. 852. See, for a detailed analysis of these appeals, paras 2-157 to 2-165, when addressing the *SAAMCO* scope of duty question.

2-068

(c) A Limited Historical Review of the Cases

(ii) Assumption of Responsibility

A practical approach to assumption of responsibility

Replace footnote 193 with:

[193] [1998] 1 W.L.R. 830 at 835G. See, also, *JP SPC 4 v Royal Bank of Scotland International* [2022] UKPC 18; [2022] 3 W.L.R. 261 (PC) (bank did not owe an investment fund a duty of care when executing a payment order made by a third-party customer). The objective test governs not only whether a duty of care exists at all, but, if it does, what tasks/responsibilities the duty embraces. One corollary of this objective approach is that the *Bolam* test has no application to these issues (see paras 2-177 to 2-197). In *Spire Property Development LLP v Withers LLP* [2022] EWCA Civ 970; [2022] P.N.L.R. 27, the appellant solicitor argued that the scope of its duty to its former client could not be wider than the relevant fee earner subjectively believed it to be, so long as that belief was one that a reasonably competent practitioner could have held. Carr LJ rejected the argument, describing it as: "a novel suggestion, unsupported by any authority to which the court was taken" (at [64]).

2-087

The notion of a "voluntary" assumption of responsibility

Replace footnote 195 with:

2-088   [195] See also the comments of Tipping J giving the judgment of New Zealand Court of Appeal in *Attorney General v Carter* [2003] 2 N.Z.L.R. 160 at [23] for a defence of the expression "deemed assumption of responsibility". See, too: *Precis (521) Plc v William M Mercer Ltd* [2004] EWCA Civ 114; [2005] P.N.L.R. 28 at [24] per Arden LJ; *Commissioners of Customs and Excise v Barclays Bank Plc* [2006] UKHL 28; [2007] 1 A.C. 181 at [5] per Lord Bingham; and *P&P Property Ltd v Owen White & Catlin LLP* [2018] EWCA Civ 1082; [2019] Ch. 273 at [76] per Patten LJ. See, too, *Spire Property Development LLP v Withers LLP* [2022] EWCA Civ 970; [2022] P.N.L.R. 27 per Carr LJ at [59].

(iv)   An Apparent Threefold Test

The cases

Replace footnote 210 with:

2-094   [210] [1995] 2 A.C. 296. For a discussion of this decision see Lord Cooke, "The Right of Spring" in P. Cane and J. Stapleton (eds), *The Law of Obligations, Essays in Celebration of John Fleming* (Oxford: Clarendon Press, 1998). Lord Cooke considers the decision in the context of the law of defamation and the law of employment. For recent coverage of the law of employment in this context, see I. Smith, Elias LJ and others (eds), *Harvey on Industrial Relations and Employment Law*, Issue 300 (London: LexisNexis, 2022).

(d)   The Modern Approach

(ii)   The Primacy of the Assumption of Responsibility Approach

Replace footnote 224 with:

2-097   [224] [2018] UKSC 43; [2018] 1 W.L.R. 4041 at [7]. All the other members of the Court agreed with Lord Sumption's judgment. See, too, *Spire Property Development LLP v Withers LLP* [2022] EWCA Civ 970; [2022] P.N.L.R. 27 per Carr LJ at [59]; and *BASF Corp v Carpmaels and Ransford* [2021] EWHC 2899 (Ch) per Adam Johnson J at [314]. In the *BASF Corp* case (allegedly negligent advice by patent attorneys), the judge rejected the claimant's attempt to establish a duty of care by analogy with the "disappointed beneficiaries" duty arising under *White v Jones* [1995] 2 A.C. 207 (HL)—see Adam Johnson J's judgment at [321].

(iv)   The Role of the Incremental Approach and the Third Limb of the Apparent Threefold Test

Replace footnote 243 with:

2-106   [243] [2018] UKSC 40; [2018] 1 W.L.R. 4021 at [23] per Lord Lloyd-Jones. See too the judgment of Lord Reed in *N v Poole BC* [2019] UKSC 25; [2020] A.C. 780 at [64]. The Privy Council endorsed this reasoning in *JP SPC 4 v Royal Bank of Scotland International* [2022] UKPC 18; [2022] 3 W.L.R. 261 (PC) (bank did not owe a duty of care to an investment fund when executing a payment order made by a third party customer)—see the judgment of Lords Hamblen and Burrows (with whom the other members of the court agreed) at [80].

(v)   The Application of the Modern Approach

Replace footnote 244 with:

2-107   [244] As was the case, for example, in *White v Jones* [1995] 2 A.C. 207 (a duty of care identified permitting a disappointed beneficiary to sue the testator's solicitor). For a detailed discussion of that case, see paras 11-046, 11-047 and 11-050 to 11-058.

   Appellate decisions in the courts of England and Wales have of course been widely criticised in the past quarter of a century or more, and compared with the approaches adopted in French and German law: see here e.g. B. Markesinis, J.M. Auby, D. Coester-Waltjen and S. Deakin, *The Tortious Liability of Statutory Bodies* (Oxford: Hart Publishing 1999); B. Markesinis, J. Bell and A. Janssen with C.P.

McGrath (eds), *Markesinis's German Law of Tort: A Comparative Treatise*, 5th edn (Oxford: Hart Publishing, 2019) and D. Leczykiewicz, *Judicial Reasoning in Tort Law: English and French Traditions Compared* (Oxford: Hart Publishing, 2021). For a general discussion of public authority negligence and duty of care, see D. Fairgrieve and D. Squires (eds), *The Negligence of Public Authorities*, 2nd edn (Oxford: Oxford University Press, 2019) Chs 1–4 and 14 especially; D. Howarth "Negligence after Murphy: Time to Rethink" (1991) 50 (1) C.L.J. 55, 85 and S. H. Bailey and M. J. Bowman, "Public authority negligence revisited" (2000) 59 (1) C.L.J. 85, 94–95. Significantly, this area of law may be important in claims against health authorities where the defence of a lack of resources is advanced: see Ch.13. It is similarly relevant in the regulated financial services sector: see Ch.14, and, for a more general discussion of regulation in this sector, J. Kirk, R. Kingham and others (eds), *Encyclopedia of Financial Services Law*, Rel.130 (London: Sweet & Maxwell, 2022).

(f) Particular Situations

(ii) Directors and Employees

Assumption of personal responsibility and reasonable reliance

Replace footnote 338 with:

[338] In cases of personal injury, directors and employees have no special protection: see, e.g. *Alder v Dickson* [1955] 1 Q.B. 158, discussed by Hobhouse LJ in *Perrett v Collins* [1998] 2 Lloyd's Rep. 255. In *Williams v Merrick* [2021] EWHC 2417 (QB), the claimant's claim against a director of an incorporated solicitors practice was struck out as disclosing no reasonable grounds for bringing the claim.

2-132

(iii) Sub-agents and Sub-contractors

Introduction

Replace footnote 353 with:

[353] P.G. Watts and F.M.B. Reynold (eds), *Bowstead & Reynolds on Agency*, 22nd edn (London: Sweet & Maxwell, 2021, 1st supp, 2021), para.5-011.

2-136

Competing considerations

Replace footnote 365 with:

[365] See *Riyad Bank v Ahli United Bank (UK) Plc* [2006] EWCA Civ 780; [2006] 2 Lloyd's Rep. 292; and *BP Plc v Aon Ltd* [2006] EWHC 424 (Comm); [2006] Lloyd's Rep. I.R. 577 per Coleman J, for cases in which, on the particular facts, it was held that the sub-contractor/sub-agent defendants owed a duty of care to the principal notwithstanding the interposition of a contractual chain. In *Avantage (Cheshire) Ltd v GB Building Solutions Ltd* [2022] EWHC 171 (TCC); [2022] P.N.L.R. 13 (claim by a PFI contractor and a local authority against sub-contractors in relation to fire safety strategy), Joanna Smith J considered that the postulated duty of care owed to the claimants was arguable notwithstanding that there was no direct contractual nexus between the parties.

2-139

5. THE SAAMCO SCOPE OF DUTY QUESTION

(c) SAAMCO's position in the analytical framework

Introduction

Replace paragraph 2-154 (to incorporate footnote updates) with:

Where in the analytical framework does the *SAAMCO* scope of duty question fit? The answer is most clearly understood by considering the position in two stages: first, following the House of Lords' decision in *SAAMCO* and until very recently; secondly, in the light of the decisions of the Supreme Court in June of 2021 in the linked appeals in *Manchester Building Society v Grant Thornton UK LLP*[399] and *Meadows v Khan.*[400]

2-154

399 [2021] UKSC 20; [2022] A.C. 783.

400 [2021] UKSC 21; [2022] A.C. 852.

The recent reappraisal by the Supreme Court

Replace paragraph 2-157 (to incorporate updates to footnotes 406 and 407) with:

2-157   In July 2021 the Supreme Court handed down its decisions in two linked appeals in *Manchester Building Society v Grant Thornton UK LLP*[406] and *Meadows v Khan*[407] (*MBS/Meadows*). In *MBS*, the claimant building society sued its auditors for incorrectly stating that it could apply hedge accounting to the manner in which it recorded the value of interest rate swaps in its financial statements. When the true position was revealed, the claimant was compelled to close out the interest rate swaps at a significant loss owing to a fall in interest rates (the MTM losses). In the Court of Appeal,[408] the case was characterised as falling into the "information" category, and the claimant's claim to recover the MTM losses failed on the basis that it could not prove it would not have suffered the same loss even had the defendant's statement as to hedge accounting represented the true position. On this basis, the *SAAMCO* counterfactual and its causal impact on the claimant's losses lay at the heart of the Court of Appeal's approach. *Meadows v Khan* concerned a GP who had negligently led the claimant to believe that she was not a carrier of the haemophilia gene. The claimant subsequently gave birth to a son with haemophilia and autism. It was accepted by the GP that the claimant would have aborted her pregnancy had she been alerted to the fact she carried the gene and that he should compensate the claimant for the costs of raising a child with haemophilia. The point of dispute concerned the extra costs of raising a child with autism. The trial judge permitted the claimant to recover the extra costs, but the Court of Appeal disagreed.

406 [2021] UKSC 20; [2022] A.C. 783.

407 [2021] UKSC 20; [2022] A.C. 783.

408 [2019] EWCA Civ 40; [2019] 1 W.L.R. 4610. The Court of Appeal dismissed the claimant's appeal from Teare J's decision at first instance that the MTM losses were not recoverable from Grant Thornton, but it did so for very different reasons to those given by Teare J at [2018] EWHC 963 (Comm); [2018] P.N.L.R. 27.

Replace footnote 409 with:

2-158   409 See, for example, *Manchester Building Society v Grant Thornton UK LLP* [2021] UKSC 20; [2022] A.C. 783 at [6] per Lords Hodge and Sales (with whom Lords Reed and Kitchin and Lady Black agreed). The judgment of Lords Hodge and Sales represents the majority view. Differing approaches were taken by Lords Leggatt and Burrows. There was the same (dis)alignment of views amongst the members of the Court in *Meadows v Khan* [2021] UKSC 21; [2022] A.C. 852.

The stage (2) scope of duty question

Replace paragraph 2-159 (to incorporate footnote updates) with:

2-159   This aspect of *SAAMCO* falls to be addressed as one of the fundamental questions as to the existence and scope of professional person A's obligations and/or duties to person B. The Supreme Court in *MBS/Meadows* described the relevant enquiry as follows:

> "In our view, the scope of the duty of care assumed by a professional adviser is governed by the purpose of the duty, judged on an objective basis by reference to the reason why the advice is being given (and, as is often the position, including in the present case, paid for)."[410]

And,

"... one looks to see what risk the duty was supposed to guard against and then looks to see whether the loss suffered represented the fruition of that risk."[411]

[410] See, for example, *Manchester Building Society v Grant Thornton UK LLP* [2021] UKSC 20; [2022] A.C. 783 at [13] per Lords Hodge and Sales.

[411] See, for example, *Manchester Building Society v Grant Thornton UK LLP* [2021] UKSC 20; [2022] A.C. 783 at [17] per Lords Hodge and Sales.

The stage (5) duty nexus question

Replace footnote 414 with:

[414] See, for example, *Manchester Building Society v Grant Thornton UK LLP* [2021] UKSC 20; [2022] A.C. 783 at [13] per Lords Hodge and Sales. For a criticism of the coherence of the stage (5) duty nexus question, see D. Howarth, "Six questions in search of a tort: has the Supreme Court transformed negligence?" (2022) 81(1) C.L.J. 20.

2-160

Does SAAMCO, as reappraised, have a causation element?

Replace footnote 415 with:

[415] [2021] UKSC 20; [2022] A.C. 783 at [13] per Lords Hodge and Sales.

2-162

(d)   Other aspects of MBS/Meadows

Reappraisal in MBS/Meadows

Replace paragraph 2-165 (to incorporate updates to footnotes 418 and 420) with:
The Supreme Court in *MBS/Meadows* described Lord Hoffmann's "information"/ "advice" dichotomy as unsatisfactory, too rigid and liable to mislead.[418] In *MBS* Lords Hodge and Sales stated:

2-165

"We welcome Lord Leggatt JSC's proposal (para 92) to dispense with the descriptions 'information' and 'advice' to be applied as terms of art in this area. As Lord Sumption JSC points out in *Hughes-Holland*,[419] para 39, both 'advice' and 'information' cases involve the giving of advice. For the reasons we give, we think it is important to link the focus of analysis of the scope of duty question and the duty nexus question back to the purpose of the duty of care assumed in the case in hand."[420]

[418] See, for example, *Manchester Building Society v Grant Thornton UK LLP* [2021] UKSC 20; [2022] A.C. 783 at [18] per Lords Hodge and Sales.

[419] *Hughes-Holland v BPE Solicitors* [2017] UKSC 21; [2018] A.C. 599.

[420] See, for example, *Manchester Building Society v Grant Thornton UK LLP* [2021] UKSC 20; [2022] A.C. 783 at [12] per Lords Hodge and Sales.

(e)   Summary of the present position

Ascertaining the nature and extent of the professional person's obligations and duties

Replace paragraph 2-167 (to incorporate updates to footnotes 421 and 422) with:
The first step is to identify the nature and extent of the express[421] and/or implied terms of any professional engagement (whether that engagement itself is express or implied) and applicable duties of care (concurrent or free-standing).[422] This will reveal what the professional person has been engaged to do or is to be taken as having agreed to do.

2-167

[421] If the professional person is under any absolute obligations, this may entitle the claimant to formulate

his claim to loss and damage on the contractual warranty measure, i.e. so as to place the claimant in the position he would have been in had the stipulated task been taken or the outcome achieved. Whilst almost all the cases involving a *SAAMCO* scope of duty analysis have concerned an obligation or duty on the part of the professional person to exercise reasonable skill and care, the scope of duty question may arise in relation to claims founded on express contractual terms, too—see *TJD Trade Ltd v BAM Construction Ltd* [2022] EWHC 1285 (TCC) per Jason Coppel QC (sitting as a Deputy High Court Judge) at [19] and [20]. See, too, *Chudley v Clydesdale Bank Plc* [2017] EWHC 2177 (Comm) (claim against bank for making payments from an account allegedly in breach of a third-party contractual arrangement) at [197] per Christopher Hancock QC (sitting as a Deputy Judge of the High Court). The Deputy Judge's decision in *Chudley* was reversed on appeal, but the Court of Appeal agreed with the approach at first instance to the *SAAMCO* question—see [2019] EWCA Civ 344; [2020] Q.B. 284 per Flaux LJ at [81] (Moylan and Longmore LJJ agreeing on this point).

[422] i.e. addressing the issues set out at sections 1 to 4 of this chapter. In the recent case of *Spire Property Development LLP v Withers LLP* [2022] EWCA Civ 970; [2022] P.N.L.R. 27, the Court of Appeal confirmed that an analysis of the extent of the professional's implied obligation and/or duty precedes, and is separate from, an analysis of the scope of that obligation/duty for the purposes of *SAAMCO*—see Carr LJ at [70]–[71].

Ascertaining the purpose of the professional person's obligations and/or duties

In paragraph 2-168, after "or selected risks.", add:

2-168   Part of this process of ascertainment entails defining the "risk" itself: whether in wider or more narrow terms.[422a]

[422a] In *Rushbond Plc v JS Design Partnership LLP* [2021] EWCA Civ 1889; [2022] P.N.L.R. 9 the respondent architect argued that, assuming it owed a duty to the owner of a disused cinema to secure the premises after an inspection, the risks falling within the duty were limited to preventing an intruder from gaining access and did not extend to the conduct of the intruder after he had gained access. In allowing the appeal, the Court of Appeal considered that, at least for the purposes of a summary judgment application, the architect's definition of the relevant "risk" was too narrow—see the judgment of Coulson LJ at [78]. See, too, the analysis of Judge Jonathan Richards (sitting as a Deputy High Court Judge) in *Aurium Real Estate London Ultra Prime Ltd v Mishcon de Reya LLP* [2022] EWHC 1253 (Ch) at [98]–[106].

Applying the SAAMCO counterfactual as a cross-check

In paragraph 2-170, after "relevant SAAMCO counterfactual.", add new footnote 422b:

2-170   [422b] In the Privy Council case of *Charles B Lawrence & Associates v Intercommercial Bank Ltd* [2021] UKPC 30; [2022] P.N.L.R. 7, the Board considered, but rejected, the outcome that would have arisen from the use of a counterfactual—see the judgment of Lord Burrows and Lady Arden (with whom the other members of the Board agreed) at [19]. By contrast, in *Richards v Speechly Bircham LLP* [2022] EWHC 935 (Comm) (claim against solicitors concerning employment advice), HHJ Russen QC considered that counterfactuals assisted the scope of duty analysis—see [472]–[475].

Burden of proof

Replace footnote 423 with:

2-171   [423] See, for example, *Manchester Building Society v Grant Thornton UK LLP* [2021] UKSC 20; [2022] A.C. 783 at [11] per Lords Hodge and Sales.

6.   THE STANDARD OF PERFORMANCE BY A PROFESSIONAL PERSON

(b)   The Meaning of Reasonable Skill and Care

The role of the courts in applying the Bolam test

Replace footnote 434 with:

2-179   [434] Conversely, if a profession adopts unduly high standards the practitioner is not necessarily negligent if he fails to comply with them: see, e.g. *United Mills Agencies Ltd v Harvey Bray & Co* [1951] 2 Lloyd's Rep. 631 at 643, col.2. For a recent example of a case where the court concluded that seemingly prevalent standards were too lax to represent a responsible body of professional opinion, see *Martlet Homes Ltd v Mullaley & Co Ltd* [2022] EWHC 1813 (TCC); 203 Con. L.R. 125 (claim against building contractor in relation to flammable cladding applied to residential tower blocks). In that case, HHJ Stephen Davies stated that the *Bolam* test was not "a get out of jail free card" and warned that "A defendant is not exonerated simply by proving that others … [were] … just as negligent" (at [271] citing Edwards-Stuart J in *199 Knightsbridge Development Ltd v WSP UK Ltd* [2014] EWHC 43 (TCC)).

7. FIDUCIARY OBLIGATIONS

(a) The Nature of Fiduciary Obligations

Introduction

Replace paragraph 2-198 (to incorporate footnote updates) with:

The contractual obligations owed by professionals are agreed by them in return for their client's promise to pay for their services. In broad terms, the law imposes a tortious duty of care on them where a client or third party is reasonably relying upon their professional skill and knowledge or where their client has retained them to confer a benefit on others. Fiduciary obligations are of a different order.[485] They are based upon the trust reposed by clients in their professional advisers, and in particular the trust that professionals will act solely in their clients' interests and not in their own. This is sometimes described as a "duty of loyalty", but in effect it amounts to an inhibition: professionals should not put themselves in a position in which their duty to act in their clients' interests is in conflict with their own interest, let alone prefer their own interests to those of their clients should there be a conflict.[486] The obligations which flow from this general prohibition are called fiduciary obligations.

2-198

[485] For a discussion on the role of a fiduciary, see Dame Sarah Worthington, *Equity*, 2nd edn (Oxford: Oxford University Press, 2006), Ch.5, 129 and following; M. Conaglen, "The Nature and Function of Fiduciary Loyalty" (2005) 121 L.Q.R. 452 and J. Edelman, "When do Fiduciary Duties Arise?" (2012) 126 L.Q.R. 302. See too, C. Mitchell, J. Harris and S. Agnew (eds), *Underhill and Hayton: Law of Trusts and Trustees*, 20th edn (London: LexisNexis, 2022), Chs 1 and 29 at paras 29.1 and following and *Lewin on Trusts* (2020), Chs 45 and 46. See too, *Chitty on Contracts* (2021) for the significance of fiduciaries in contract.

[486] See, e.g. the formulation by Millett LJ in *Bristol & West Building Society v Mothew* [1998] Ch. 1 at 18B–18C:

> "The distinguishing obligation of a fiduciary is the obligation of loyalty. The principal is entitled to the single-minded loyalty of his fiduciary. This core liability has several facets. A fiduciary must act in good faith; he must *not* make a profit out of his trust; he must not place himself in a position where his duty and his interest may conflict; he may *not* act for his own benefit or the benefit of a third person without the informed consent of his principal." (emphasis added)

See also *Attorney General v Blake* [1998] Ch. 439 at 455, where Lord Woolf MR giving the judgment of the Court of Appeal (himself and Millett and Mummery LJJ) said at 455E:

> "… equity is proscriptive, not prescriptive: see *Breen v Williams* (1996) 186 C.L.R. 71. It tells the fiduciary what he must not do. It does not tell him what he ought to do."

So it is wrong to talk of a fiduciary owing a duty of disclosure. Disclosure of a fiduciary's interest is a defence, not a duty: *Blackmagic Design Pty v Overliese* [2011] FCAFC 24; (2011) 276 A.L.R. 646 at [106]–[108] per Besanko J with whom the other members of the Federal Court of Australia, Full Court, agreed. In *A Company v Secretariat Consulting Pte Ltd* [2021] EWCA Civ 6; [2021] 4 W.L.R. 20, Coulson LJ stated that: "There appears to be a general acceptance … that a fiduciary duty may – depending on the facts – be owed by a professional to his or her client" (at [48]). In that case, the Court of Appeal considered, obiter, that a fiduciary duty of loyalty may be owed by "a provider or litigation support services/expert" to a client, but this would depend on the facts (see the judgment of Coulson LJ at [66]).

Effect of fiduciary obligations on contractual obligations and tortious duties

Replace footnote 501 with:

2-201   [501]   *Nornberg v Wynrib* [1992] 2 S.C.R. 226 per Sopinka J at 272; quoted with approval in *Pilmer v Duke Group Ltd* [2001] 2 B.C.L.C. 773 at 733c–733d. Particular care is needed if the claimant is seeking to impose fiduciary duties upon a professional prior to the time at which the contract of engagement has been executed or after the time it has come to an end. For an example of a judge's rejection of the claimant's case that a fiduciary duty arose on the part of a solicitor after the engagement had come to an end, see *Al-Subaihi v Al-Sanea* [2021] EWHC 2609 (Comm) (the successful appeal at [2022] EWCA Civ 1349 did not relate to this point). See too *Gray v Smith* [2022] EWHC 1153 (Ch), per Mr Recorder Richard Smith at [388].

The significance of the retainer

Replace footnote 521 with:

2-205   [521]   [1993] A.C. 205. The reverse may also be true. The courts may prefer to consider duties of loyalty and conflict, on the part of a professional, as more naturally arising out of the contractual engagement with the client rather than as a freestanding creature of equity—see *A Company v Secretariat Consulting Pte Ltd* [2021] EWCA Civ 6; [2021] 4 W.L.R. 20.

8.   CONFIDENTIALITY

(b)   Origins of the Duty of Confidence

A free-standing equitable duty

Replace footnote 634 with:

2-241   [634]   See also *Toulson and Phipps on Confidentiality* (2020), paras 2-101 to 2-103.

(c)   Elements of the Cause of Action

Confidentiality of the information

Replace footnote 639 with:

2-243   [639]   *Attorney General v Guardian Newspapers Ltd (No.2)* [1990] 1 A.C. 109 at 215B per Bingham LJ referring to Gurry, at p.70. See also *Toulson and Phipps on Confidentiality* (2020), para.3-109.

Misuse

Replace footnote 655 with:

2-247   [655]   *Warren v DSG Retail Ltd* [2021] EWHC 2168 (QB); [2021] E.M.L.R. 25.

CHAPTER 3

REMEDIES

2. DAMAGES

Banque Bruxelles Lambert SA v Eagle Star Insurance Co Ltd

Replace footnote 21 with:

[21] [2021] UKSC 20; [2021] 3 W.L.R. 81. The Supreme Court approved the decision and the reasoning of the Court of Appeal (as interpreted by the Supreme Court) in *AssetCo Plc v Grant Thornton UK LLP* [2020] EWCA Civ 1151; [2021] 3 All E.R. 517. See also *Charles B Lawrence & Associates v Intercommercial Bank Ltd (Trinidad and Tobago)* [2021] UKPC 30; [2022] P.N.L.R. 7 and *Aurium Real Estate London Ultra Prime Ltd v Mishcon de Reya LLP* [2022] EWHC 1253 (Ch).

3-005

4. EQUITABLE REMEDIES

(a) Rescission

3-015 *Replace heading footnote 51 with:* A full discussion of equitable remedies is beyond the scope of this book. See I.C.F. Spry, *The Principles of Equitable Remedies*, 9th edn (London: Sweet & Maxwell, 2014); J. McGhee, S. Elliott and others (eds), *Snell's Equity*, 34th edn (London: Sweet & Maxwell, 2020, 3rd supp, 2022); and J.D. Heydon, M.J. Leeming, and P.G. Turner, Meagher, Gummow & Lehane, *Equity, Doctrines and Remedies*, 5th edn (Sydney: LexisNexis Butterworths, 2014). Remedies such as specific performance and rectification are not considered at all, since they are rarely sought in claims against professional persons.

5. INTEREST

(a) Interest on Damages under the Senior Courts Act 1981

(i) General

Replace heading footnote 90 with: See the helpful notes and commentary at Section 16AI of Lord Justice Coulson and others (eds), *The White Book: Civil Procedure 2022* (London: Sweet & Maxwell 2022)

6. THE CONSUMER RIGHTS ACT 2015

Replace footnote 105 with:

3-031 [105] See paras 2-057 to 2-060. See also, for further discussion, G. Woodroffe, C. Willett and C. Twigg-Flesner, *Woodroffe & Lowe Consumer Law and Practice*, 10th edn (London: Sweet & Maxwell, 2016).

CHAPTER 4

CONTRIBUTION BETWEEN DEFENDANTS

3. LIABILITY OF THE PERSON CLAIMING CONTRIBUTION

Replace paragraph 4-006 (to incorporate updates to footnotes 15 and 16) with:

Finally, until recently the position appeared to be that the wording of the proviso **4-006** in s.1(4) of the Civil Liability (Contribution) Act 1978 ("provided, however, that he would have been liable assuming that the factual basis of the claim against him could be established") was wide enough to allow a person against whom contribution is sought to dispute that claim on the basis that the person seeking to recover contribution had a collateral defence which it would have been for him, and not the original claimant, to establish (namely a defence which depended on facts which were not inconsistent with the facts pleaded by the original claimant and required to be assumed under the proviso, such as limitation).[14] The Court of Appeal has held that this is not the case.[15] The purpose of the s.1(4) proviso is to prohibit any inquiry into whether the party seeking contribution was not actually liable to the claimant. All the party seeking contribution needs to do is show that, on the assumption that the factual basis of the claim against him could be established, such factual basis discloses a reasonable cause of action in law against him so as to make him liable to the claimant.[16]

---

[14] *BRB (Residuary) Ltd v Connex South Eastern Ltd* [2008] EWHC 1172 (QB); [2008] 1 W.L.R. 2867, Cranston J, following *Arab Monetary Fund v Hashim, Times,* 17 June 1993, Chadwick J. Cranston J considered himself bound to follow this decision.

[15] *WH Newson Holding Ltd v IMI Plc* [2016] EWCA Civ 773; [2017] Ch. 27. The Court of Appeal (per Sir Colin Rimer) held that a Pt 20 defendant could not resist the contribution claim on the grounds that the defendant was not, or would not have been, liable to the claimant because the claim against it was time barred. However, it is important to note that *Newson* concerned the situation where liability on the part of the defendant to the contribution claim had already been established. An attempt to rely on *Newson* to argue that s.1(4) of the Act obviated the need for the party seeking contribution to prove that

the party from whom contribution was sought was (him or herself) negligent was given short shrift by the Court of Appeal in *Percy v Merriman White* [2022] EWCA Civ 493; [2022] 3 W.L.R. 1.

[16] The Court of Appeal considered *Hashim* at length and decided that, in so far as *Hashim* decided that the party against whom contribution was sought was permitted to raise an inquiry as to whether, in light of any collateral defence raised by the party seeking contribution to the claimant's claim, he would not have been actually liable to the claimant, it was wrongly decided.

(a) Basis of Liability

Replace footnote 18 with:

4-007 [18] [2002] UKHL 14; [2002] 1 W.L.R. 1397 at [33]. Lord Steyn accepted the criticisms of the decision of the Court of Appeal in *Friends' Provident Life Office v Hillier Parker May & Rowden* [1997] Q.B. 85 made in *Goff & Jones, The Law of Restitution*, 5th edn (London: Sweet & Maxwell, 1998), p.396: a claim in restitution is not for "damage suffered" by the claimant, but in respect of the unjust enrichment of the defendant. See too the most recent edition: C. Mitchell, P. Mitchell and S. Watterson (eds), *Goff & Jones, The Law of Unjust Enrichment*, 9th edn (London: Sweet & Maxwell, 2016) (10th edn forthcoming, 2022). It is not a claim for compensation and so does not fall within s.1(1). At [26] Lord Steyn also stated that the 1978 Act was intended to extend the reach of the contribution principle to a wider range of cases than before.

CHAPTER 5

DEFENCES

1. EXCLUSION OR RESTRICTION OF LIABILITY

Replace footnote 2 with:

5-001 [2] For a brief history on recent reforms in the legal and healthcare professions, for example, see I. Miller and others (eds), *Cordery on Legal Services*, 9th edn, Issue 129 (London: LexisNexis, 2022), Div. A–D, and D. Gomez and others (eds), *The Regulation of Healthcare Professionals: Law, Principle and Process*, 2nd edn (London: Sweet & Maxwell, 2019), Ch.1.

(a) The Position at Common Law

Replace list in paragraph 5-006 (to incorporate updates to footnotes 18 and 19) with:

5-006
1. if a contractual term is relied upon, it is expressly incorporated into the contract of engagement[18];
2. if a notice is relied upon, it was drawn to the client's attention; and
3. in either case, the wording used is sufficiently clear to apply to negligence.[19]

[18] As to which, see H. Beale and others (eds), *Chitty on Contracts*, 34th edn, Vol.1 (London: Sweet & Maxwell, 2021), Ch.15, paras 15-005 to 15-015.

[19] As to which, see *Chitty on Contracts* (2021), Ch.15, para.15-012. By far the safest way of excluding or restricting liability for negligence is to use the word "negligence" or some synonym for it. See, generally *Smith v South Wales Switchgear Co Ltd* [1978] 1 W.L.R. 165 and *Photo Production Ltd v Securicor Transport Ltd* [1980] A.C. 827.

Replace footnote 20 with:

5-007 [20] *Chitty on Contracts* (2021), Ch.17, paras 17-008 and 17-009.

Replace footnote 26 with:

5-009 [26] See the authorities referred to in paras 12.41 to 12.43 of Lewison, *The Interpretation of Contracts* (2020) and *Chitty on Contracts* (2021), Ch.17, paras 17-007 to 17-014.

(b) The Statutory Framework

Unfair Contract Terms Act 1977

Replace footnote 49 with:

5-017 [49] The operation of s.11 is briefly discussed by the House of Lords in *George Mitchell (Chesterhall) Ltd v Finney Lock Seeds Ltd* [1983] 2 A.C. 803 at 815–816. J. Adams and R. Brownsword review the earlier authorities in "The Unfair Contract Terms Act: A Decade of Discretion" in (1988) 104 L.Q.R. 94. They criticise the *George Mitchell* decision as having given rise to undue uncertainty. For a general discussion of the "reasonableness" test, see *Chitty on Contracts* (2021), Ch.17, paras 17-099 to 17-115.

The requirement of reasonableness

Replace footnote 56 with:

5-018 [56] The availability of insurance may also be a relevant factor in applying the test of reasonableness under s.11(1) (although it is not a relevant factor that the party seeking to limit or exclude liability has or has not in fact obtained insurance): see *Chitty on Contracts* (2021), Ch.17, para.17-103, fn.625 for the relevant authorities.

Replace footnote 61 with:

[61] A necessary precondition to the application of s.3 of the Unfair Contract Terms Act 1977, which applies to liability in contracts either (i) made before 1 October 2015 where either one party deals "as a consumer" or (ii) contracts made on the other party's written standard terms of business. As to the former see *R&B Customs Brokers Co Ltd v United Dominions Trust* [1988] 1 W.L.R. 321 CA and *Chitty on Contracts* (2021), Ch.17, para.17-072. For the position for contracts made with consumers on or after 1 October 2015 see paras 5-027 to 5-031.

5-020

Unfair Terms in Consumer Contracts Regulations 1999

Replace footnote 69 with:

[69] Directive 93/13 which is discussed in *Chitty on Contracts* (2021), Ch.40, para.40-225.

5-023

Replace footnote 71 with:

[71] reg.3(1). This is not the same as "dealing as a consumer" for the purposes of the Unfair Contract Terms Act 1977 (as to which see para.5-021): see *Chitty on Contracts* (2021), Ch.40, paras 40-031 to 40-051 for a full discussion of the various definitions of "consumer".

5-024

Replace paragraph 5-026 (to incorporate deletion of text after "question is made" and footnote 81) with:

The test of fairness has been held to be a composite test covering both the making and the substance of the contract.[78] A term is unfair if it causes a significant imbalance in the rights of the parties which is contrary to the requirements of good faith. A "significant imbalance" will occur when the term tilts the parties' contractual rights and obligations in favour of the supplier. The requirements of "good faith" have not, prior to the Regulations, been recognised in the law of contract save for in particular circumstances (such as contracts of insurance). The House of Lords has held that in the context of the Regulations the concept of "good faith" was not an artificial or technical concept but connoted fair and open dealing.[79] In assessing the fairness of the term it would appear that an objective test is to be applied by considering the position of typical parties when the contract in question is made.[80]

5-026

[78] *Director General of Fair Trading v First National Bank Plc* [2001] UKHL 52; [2002] 1 A.C. 481 at [17] per Lord Bingham. See also *Bryen & Langley Ltd v Martin Boston* [2005] EWCA Civ 973; [2005] B.L.R. 508.

[79] *Director General of Fair Trading v First National Bank Plc* [2001] UKHL 52; [2002] 1 A.C. 481 at [17].

[80] *Director General of Fair Trading v First National Bank Plc* [2001] UKHL 52; [2002] 1 A.C. 481 at [20].

(c)   Exclusion of Liability to Third Parties

Contracts (Rights of Third Parties) Act 1999

Replace footnote 114 with:

[114] See *Chitty on Contracts* (2021), Ch.17, para.17-046.

5-033

2. LIMITATION IN CONTRACT AND TORT

(a) The Limitation Period

Replace paragraph 5-036 (to incorporate updates to footnotes 120 and 121) with:

5-036   Under the Limitation Act 1980 claims founded on tort[120] or simple contract[121] are barred after the expiration of six years from the date on which the cause of action accrues.[122] In the case of persons under a disability (defined as infants or persons of unsound mind)[123] "the action may be brought at any time before the expiration of six years from the date when he ceased to be under a disability or died (whichever first occurred)".[124] The limitation period is also extended in cases of fraud, concealment or mistake.[125]

[120] Limitation Act 1980 s.2. A claim under s.2(1) of the Misrepresentation Act 1967 is "an action founded on tort" and so falls within s.2 of the Limitation Act 1980: *Green v Eadie* [2011] EWHC B24 (Ch); [2012] Ch. 363 (Mark Cawson QC, sitting as a Deputy High Court Judge). For a general discussion of limitation of actions in tort, see A. McGee, *Limitation Periods*, 9th edn (London: Sweet & Maxwell, 2022) and A. Tettenborn and others (eds), *Clerk & Lindsell on Torts*, 23rd edn (London: Sweet & Maxwell, 2020, 2nd supp, 2022), Ch.31. For an overview of limitation of actions in general and proposals for reform, see The Law Commission, *Limitation of Actions*, Law Com. No.270 (London: The Law Commission, 2001), paras 2.97–2.99. This book is concerned only with limitation in the context of professional liability.

[121] Limitation Act 1980 s.5. For a general discussion of limitation of actions in contract, see McGee, *Limitation Periods* (2022), *Chitty on Contracts* (2021), Ch.31 and The Law Commission, *Limitation of Actions*, Law Com. No.270 (London: The Law Commission, 2001). Claims based on a specialty (i.e. a contract under seal) have a limitation period of 12 years: Limitation Act 1980 s.8.

[122] The fact that time is running for breach by a professional in respect of one retainer or transaction does not mean that time is also running in respect of a similar or identical breach of another retainer or a different transaction. So in *St Anselm Development Co v Slaughter & May (A Firm)* [2013] EWHC 125 (Ch) (David Richards J) solicitors were retained to act in relation to the leases of two flats in the same building. A failure to give relevant advice in relation to the lease of the first property was a separate cause of action for the subsequent failure to give the same advice in relation to the second property.

[123] Limitation Act 1980 s.38(2). An "infant" is a person under 18: see Family Law Reform Act 1969 s.1. For the definition of "unsound mind", see Limitation Act 1980 s.38(2) and (3).

[124] Limitation Act 1980 s.28(1).

[125] See paras 5-133 to 5-139.

(c) Date when Cause of Action in Tort Accrues

(i) Claims against Solicitors

Previous action dismissed for want of prosecution

Replace footnote 212 with:

5-059   [212] [2020] EWCA Civ 851; [2020] 1 W.L.R. 4638. See, to the same effect: *Christie v The Mary Ward Legal Centre* [2022] EWHC 1684 (QB).

Where the client purchases a property

Replace footnote 213 with:

5-060   [213] See para.5-063. See also *Sullavan v Teare* [2010] QCA 70; [2011] 1 Qd.R. 291: a claim against solicitors: cause of action in tort complete when the claimant was contractually committed to pay more than the property was worth, following *HTW Valuers (Central Qld) Pty Ltd v Astonland Pty Ltd* [2004] HCA 54; (2004) 217 C.L.R. 640, (a claim against valuers). Market value is the measure, even if the claimant does not intend to sell the property: *Elliott v Hattens Solicitors* [2021] EWCA Civ 720; [2021] P.N.L.R. 25.

Omissions capable of being remedied

Replace footnote 216 with:

[216] But where a solicitor's error can no longer possibly be put right, time begins to run, even if, in relation to a claim of mishandled legal proceedings, the time when it becomes impossible to remedy the situation occurs during the proceedings, rather than at their conclusion: *Holt v Holley and Steer Solicitors* [2020] EWCA Civ 851; [2020] 1 W.L.R. 4638. Further, each separate failure over the course of a lawyer-client relationship is treated separately for limitation purposes: see *Sciortino v Beaumont* [2021] EWCA Civ 786; [2021] Ch. 365.

5-061

(d) Effect of the Latent Damage Act 1986

(iv) The Other Facts Relevant to the Current Action

Damage was attributable in whole or in part to the act or omission which is alleged to constitute negligence

Replace footnote 384 with:

[384] *Nash v Eli Lilly & Co* [1993] 1 W.L.R. 782 at 797A–798A per Purchas LJ, giving the judgment of the Court of Appeal. On the contrary, a claimant who has "no reason to suspect" that that there had been flawed advice or flawed omissions from advice was not fixed with knowledge in *Witcomb v J Keith Park Solicitors* [2021] EWHC 2038 (QB); [2021] P.N.L.R. 24 at [83] (Bourne J).

5-106

(vi) The 15-year Long Stop

Replace footnote 426 with:

[426] *Financial Services Compensation Scheme Ltd v Larnell (Insurances) Ltd (In Creditors' Voluntary Liquidation)* [2005] EWCA Civ 1408; [2006] Q.B. 808. That said, an amendment to a claim to introduce allegations pre-dating the 15-year period was not permitted in *Cameron Taylor Consulting Ltd v BDW Trading Ltd* [2022] EWCA Civ 31; [2022] P.N.L.R. 11.

5-118

3. LIMITATION IN EQUITY

Replace footnote 496 with:

[496] For a fuller discussion of limitation in the context of claims for equitable relief, see: I.C.F. Spry, *The Principles of Equitable Remedies*, 9th edn (London: Sweet & Maxwell, 2014), pp.251–253 and 431–446; J. McGhee, S. Elliott and others (eds), Snell's *Equity*, 34th edn (London: Sweet & Maxwell, 2020, 2nd supp, 2022), Ch.5, para.5-116 and Ch.30, 30-073—30-089 and The Law Commission, *Limitation of Actions*, Law Com. No.270 (London: The Law Commission, 2001), paras 2.39–2.47 and 2.52–2.66 (and proposals for reform at paras 4.94–4.137 and 4.158–4.196). The equitable doctrines of laches and acquiescence are discussed separately, at paras 5-168 to 5-180.

5-140

(a) Express Application of the Limitation Act 1980

Replace paragraph 5-145 (to incorporate new text and footnote) with:

This provision clearly applies to an action based upon a fraudulent breach of trust or to recover trust property or its proceeds from a trustee implicated in the fraud in some way.[501a] In recent years, there have been attempts to extend its effect to other claims.[502]

5-145

[501a] To be distinguished from a co-trustee (such as a fellow member of a solicitors' partnership) who is not implicated in the fraud, as the Court of Appeal held was the case in respect of *Dixon, Coles & Gill (A Former Firm) v Baines* [2021] EWCA Civ 1097; [2022] Ch. 195. See at [45] (Sir Timothy Lloyd).

[502] A claim against a company director who has acquired and disposed of the company's property is a

claim against him as a trustee and falls within s.21(1)(b): *JJ Harrison (Properties Ltd) v Harrison* [2001] EWCA Civ 1467; [2002] 1 B.C.L.C. 162. However, a claim against a company director for an account of secret or unauthorised profits does not, because there was no pre-existing fiduciary responsibility for the relevant property (i.e. the profits): see *Gwembe Valley Development Co Ltd v Koshy (No.3)* [2003] EWCA Civ 1048; [2004] 1 B.C.L.C. 131 at [119].

(b) Application of the Limitation Act 1980 by Analogy

Replace footnote 550 with:

5-163 [550] See J.W. Brunyate, *Limitation of Actions in Equity* (London: Stevens & Sons, 1932), p.17.

6. ILLEGALITY

In paragraph 5-194, after "causa non oritur", replace "action" with:

5-194 actio

Replace footnote 646 with:

5-195 [646] *Patel v Mirza* [2016] UKSC 42; [2017] A.C. 467. See here S. Green and A. Bogg (eds), *Illegality after Patel v Mirza* (Oxford: Hart Publishing, 2018).

CHAPTER 6

LITIGATION

1. GROUP ACTIONS

(a) General

Replace paragraph 6-001 (to incorporate updates to footnotes 4 and 10) with:

Group actions, also known as multi-party actions, and as class actions in other **6-001** jurisdictions, concern the litigation of a number of claims having some similarity, usually the same claimant or defendants and similar legal and factual issues, which are administered together by the same judge. There has been an upsurge in group actions since the 1980s. They may cover a large variety of types of claims, including actions against employers for personal injury,[1] litigation alleging cancer from industrial plants,[2] transport disaster claims,[3] claims for environmental nuisance,[4] perhaps most well-known of all a number of pharmaceutical product liability claims,[5] other product liability actions,[6] claims against arms of the state for negligence causing personal injury,[7] claims challenging mortgages and bank charges,[8] and claims for financial loss by investors from alleged negligent misstatements in prospectuses.[9] There have also been a number of professional negligence group actions, which will be briefly considered below. As a result of all this litigation, there has been a great deal of experience in how to manage and litigate group actions. Some of it is reflected in reported decisions and in the provisions for group

[27]

actions in the Civil Procedure Rules 1998 (CPR), but many of the techniques are necessarily of a more informal kind which is best found in the leading books on the subject.[10]

[1] The British Coal Vibration White Finger Litigation and the Respiratory Disease Litigation, which mostly resulted in success for the claimants.

[2] The Sellafield childhood leukaemia cases, which failed on causation in *Reay and Hope v British Nuclear Fuels Plc* (1994) 5 Med. L.R. 1.

[3] See, e.g. the *Herald of Free Enterprise* disaster of 1987 (where three arbitrators set landmark awards for post-traumatic stress disorder), and the Hillsborough football stadium disaster of 1989.

[4] The Docklands Nuisance actions (some of which settled, some of which were withdrawn); the Corby Group Litigation (see *Corby Group Litigation v Corby DC* [2009] EWHC 1944 (TCC); [2010] Env. L.R. D2); Westmill Landfill Group Litigation (see *Barr v Biffa Waste Services Ltd* [2011] EWHC 1003 (TCC); [2011] 4 All E.R. 1065; 137 Con. L.R. 125); Ocensa Pipeline Group Litigation (*Arroyo v Equion Energia Ltd* [2016] EWHC 1699 (TCC)); litigation arising from the collapse of the Fundao dam in south-eastern Brazil (originally struck out and later reinstated: see *Municipio De Mariana v BHP Group (UK) Ltd* [2022] EWCA Civ 951).

[5] The Pertussis Vaccine Litigation (see *Loveday v Renton* [1989] 1 Med. L.R. 117, where the case effectively ended with failure by the claimants on a preliminary issue on causation); the Opren Litigation (where proceedings were discontinued); the Myodil Litigation (where a core cohort achieved settlements), the large and expensively unsuccessful Benzodiazepine Litigation; the Norplant Litigation (where legal aid was withdrawn shortly before trial) and the Hepatitis C Litigation where the claimants succeeded at trial (reported as *A v National Blood Authority* [2001] 3 All E.R. 289). In many of these cases, causation has been the key issue on which the claimants failed.

[6] See, e.g. the Tobacco Litigation, which ended in failure for the claimants following a preliminary issue on limitation; the litigation against Volkswagen Group companies arising from the diesel emissions scandal of 2015.

[7] The HIV Haemophiliac Litigation, which was settled following a preliminary hearing in the Court of Appeal (reported at [1996] P.N.L.R. 290); the Creutzfeldt-Jakob Disease Litigation, where the claimants succeeded in establishing liability (reported at [1996] 7 Med. L.R. 309); the Iraqi Civilian Litigation (concerning allegations of abuse by British military personnel in Iraq between 2003 and 2009) (see [2016] UKSC 25; [2016] 1 W.L.R. 2001); the Mau Mau group actions against the Foreign and Commonwealth Office arising out of the conduct of the British Colonial Administration in Kenya.

[8] e.g. the Shared Appreciation Mortgage Group Litigation.

[9] e.g. the RBS Rights Issue Litigation.

[10] See D. Grave, M. McIntosh and G. Rowan, *Class Actions in England and Wales* (London: Sweet & Maxwell, 2018), C. Hodges, *Multi-Party Actions* (Oxford: Oxford University Press, 2001) (2nd edn by C. Hodges and G. Webb (eds) forthcoming, 2024) and M. Day, P. Balen, and G. McCool, *Multi-Party Actions* (London: LAG, 1995). While the latter was written long before the introduction of the Civil Procedure Rules, it still provides valuable insights, and it includes helpful pleadings and orders in the appendices.

(c) Procedure

Replace paragraph 6-003 (to incorporate updates to footnotes 16 and 24 and new footnote 26a) with:

6-003   CPR Pt 19 rr.10–15, and the accompanying Practice Direction on Group Litigation (PD 19B), are concerned with group litigation. No similar body of rules existed before 2000. The rules can be summarised as follows. A court can make a Group Litigation Order (GLO), where there are, or are likely to be, a number of claims giving rise to common or related issues of fact or law ("the GLO issues").[16] A GLO must[17] contain directions about the establishment of a register,[18] specify the GLO issues to identify the claims, and identify a management court.[19] Judgments or orders in one claim within the group action are generally binding on other claims.[20]

Directions may be given[21] varying the GLO issues, providing for test claims to proceed,[22] appointing lead solicitors,[23] specifying what is to be included in a statement of case,[24] and providing for a cut-off-date for joining the litigation[25] and for publicising the GLO.[26] Co-ordinated litigation may be carried out outside the framework of GLOs in appropriate cases, for instance by the use of representative actions.[26a]

[16] CPR rr.19.10 and 19.11(1). No guidance is given in the rules as to how the court should exercise the discretion. The Practice Direction at paras 2.1–3.9 sets out a number of preliminary steps which must be undertaken before applying for a GLO, the information required for making an application, and which judges must approve any order. Before a GLO is made, common or related issues should be agreed or identified with sufficient specificity, and the court may defer making a GLO until that has been done: see *Alame v Royal Dutch Shell Plc* [2022] EWHC 989 (TCC).

[17] CPR r.19.11(2).

[18] While para.6.5 of the Practice Direction envisages that this will normally be kept by the court, it may well be more convenient for a lead solicitor to do so. In accordance with established law, a GLO will provide that a person becomes a party on the date of entry to the group register. This had a significant effect in *Kimathi v Foreign and Commonwealth Office* [2016] EWHC 3005 (QB); [2017] 1 W.L.R. 1081, where one claimant had died after the issue of proceedings but before his name was added to the register. The court held that his claim was a nullity which was not capable of being cured.

[19] There will usually be a managing judge who will conduct all hearings. This can give rise to an argument that a judge who has expressed views on the evidence in one hearing should recuse him or herself from conducting future hearings on the ground of apparent predetermination. In *Bates v Post Office Ltd (No.4)* [2019] EWHC 871 (QB), Fraser J refused such an application to recuse himself, citing authority that judges ought not to be too ready to accede to such applications in group litigation.

[20] CPR r.19.12.

[21] CPR r.19.13. In *Viner v Volkswagen Group UK Ltd* [2018] EWHC 2006 (QB), the court rejected applications to extend time for service of claim forms which were based on the argument that service had been delayed pending discussion of how to include the claims within the group litigation. The appropriate course would have been to serve the claim forms and seek a stay if necessary to discuss whether and how the claims should be included.

[22] See also para.15 of the Practice Direction. In selecting test cases, the aim should be to ensure that issues common to all claimants (as to which a judgment may bind all claimants) are resolved and that other factual and legal issues are decided in the context of test cases in such a way as to promote settlement of claims in the group: see *Lancaster v Peacock* [2020] EWHC 1231 (Ch) at [2]–[3].

[23] This is a necessary provision of last resort. Selection of a lead solicitor is almost always voluntary. Para.2.2 of the Practice Direction assists in this process. In *Hutson v Tata Steel* [2017] EWHC 2647 (QB); [2017] 6 Costs L.O. 753, the court refused an application to add an additional firm of solicitors as a lead firm within a group action, where the application was strongly resisted by the existing lead solicitors, and it was clear that an increase in the number of lead solicitors would add to the overall expense of the litigation, as well as the demands on the court's own resources. In *Lungowe v Vedanta Resources Plc* [2020] EWHC 749 (TCC); [2020] B.L.R. 410, the court was faced with an application for a GLO made in respect of three separate sets of proceedings where the claimants were represented by two firms of solicitors. At [38], Fraser J held the following three principles to be applicable in that situation. First, parties to litigation are generally entitled to be represented by the solicitors of their choice and to have their case argued by their own representatives. However, in group litigation, that entitlement is qualified. In order properly to achieve efficient conduct and case management of the group litigation, that basic right takes second place to the advancement of the rights of the cohort. This is achieved through the role of the lead solicitor, and the use of counsel chosen and instructed by the lead solicitor. Secondly, the relationship between the lead solicitor and other firms has to be carefully defined in writing. In the absence of agreement, or in the event of deficiency in that agreement, the court will become involved. That is a reserve power and will be used only rarely. Thirdly, in group litigation the claimants would be entitled to instruct one counsel team only. Different groups of claimants are not entitled to instruct different groups of counsel. The court also reiterated at [42] the importance of co-operation between the parties in group litigation, pursuant to rr.1.4(2)(a) and 1.3 of the CPR.

[24] There is often provision for "Master pleadings", and para.14.1 of the Practice Direction envisages that "Group Particulars of Claim" may be provided. Individual claim forms are required to be issued

by each claimant, under para.6.1A of the Practice Direction. However, they need only be "the simplest of documents", identifying the nature of the claim in general terms. Issues will be identified in detail by the GLO and Master Pleadings. See *Boake Allen Ltd v Revenue and Customs Commissioners* [2007] UKHL 25; [2007] 1 W.L.R. 1386 at [28]–[32] per Lord Woolf. In group litigation, parties are under the usual obligation to plead the facts necessary to make their case, so that each claimant must plead sufficient facts to complete that person's cause of action, although this may be done by schedules or other documents annexed to the group pleading: see *Alame v Royal Dutch Shell Plc* [2022] EWHC 989 (TCC).

[25] CPR r.19.13(e). The exercise of the power to set and extend such cut-off dates is pragmatic and fact-sensitive. See *Greenwood v Goodwin* [2014] EWHC 227 (Ch); *Holloway v Transform Medical Group (CS) Ltd* [2014] EWHC 1641 (QB); *Pearce v Secretary of State for Energy and Climate Change* [2015] EWHC 3775 (QB); and *Weaver v British Airways Plc* [2021] EWHC 217 (QB); [2021] Costs L.R. 121. In *Holloway*, the court held that where a claimant had failed to apply to join a group litigation register by a cut-off date set in court directions and sought to join out of time, it was necessary for her to satisfy the criteria for relief from sanctions under CPR r.3.9. The argument that the sanction did not apply to her because she was not a party to the group litigation at the time when the order was made was rejected. An application for relief from sanction of this kind failed in the Mau Mau group action, where the claimant applying to be added to the register was doing so two-and-a-half years after it had closed and the reason for the lateness of the application was not entirely clear: see *Kimathi v Foreign and Commonwealth Office* [2017] EWHC 939 (QB). In *Hutson v Tata Steel UK Ltd* [2019] EWHC 143 (QB), the court acceded to an application to extend time where cases had not entered the register in time, in view of the fact that this would not substantially prejudice the defendant or be disruptive of the proceedings. The court also decided that it had power to extend time where cases had been entered on the register before the deadline but without the requisite formalities having actually been satisfied. In that case and in *Crossley v Volkswagen AG* [2019] EWHC 698 (QB), the courts considered applications to add cases after cut-off dates as applications for relief from sanction. *Crossley* was a striking example, in that permission was given for over 5,000 cases to be added. However, the number was modest in the context of the case and the claimants had been named on the original claim form.

[26] See also para.13 of the Practice Direction.

[26a] The representative procedure under CPR r.19.6 was considered in a large class claim brought against the internet search engine provider, Google LLC: see *Lloyd v Google LLC* [2021] UKSC 50; [2021] 3 W.L.R. 1268. This procedure requires all members of the represented class to have the same interest, so that there can be no conflict of interest, but it does not require the consent of all class members.

Replace paragraph 6-004 (to incorporate new text and footnote) with:

6-004   The rules only lay down, and can only lay down, a very broad framework, as the circumstances of potential group actions can be very diverse. A wide range of procedural tools is available to the court, and the procedure can cope with litigation on a vast scale.[26b] The first question will be whether a GLO should be made, and orders may be refused where actions would more efficiently or fairly be resolved by being consolidated or by representative actions or lead cases being ordered to be heard.[27] A GLO may also be refused where funding for claims is evidently lacking or the factual foundations of the claims are speculative.[28] If a GLO is made, case management will be tailored to the circumstances of the dispute.[29] A fundamental issue in many cases is likely to be whether the group action should progress by deciding generic issues without investigating any or many individual cases first, or whether individual cases should be properly pleaded and scrutinised before deciding on which generic issues should be tried.[30] In general, a high degree of co-operation is required between the lawyers for the opposing sides,[31] and judges have had to be active[32] and interventionist in these type of actions long before the Woolf reforms. Solicitors for claimants in group litigation are expected to behave professionally when advertising for and recruiting additional claimants.[33]

[26b] See *Municipio De Mariana v BHP Group (UK) Ltd* [2022] EWCA Civ 951, where the Court of Appeal held that it had been wrong to strike out claims of 200,000 claimants resulting from the collapse of the Fundao dam. The fact that an otherwise proper claim was on a vast scale and said to be

"unmanageable" did not make it an abuse of process. In any event, the claim was not unmanageable within the GLO procedure.

[27] See para.2.3 of the Practice Direction; *Hobson v Ashton Morton Slack Solicitors* [2006] EWHC 1134 (Admin).

[28] See *Austin v Miller Argent (South Wales) Ltd* [2011] EWCA Civ 928; [2011] Env. L.R. 32. Or the issues may not be sufficiently common or sufficiently related to make a GLO. See *Various v Barking, Havering and Redbridge University Hospitals NHS Trust* QBD unreported 21 May 2014.

[29] In general terms, the fact that a person is a claimant in group litigation, but not a test claimant, does not prevent the person from successfully making an application for an interim payment of damages, if the conditions for such a payment are met. However, there may be terms of specific GLOs which preclude this form of interim relief. See *Test Claimants in the FII Group Litigation v Revenue and Customs Comrs* [2012] EWCA Civ 57; [2012] 1 W.L.R. 2375 at [47]; *GKN Holdings Plc v Revenue and Customs Commissioners* [2013] EWHC 108 (Ch); [2013] B.T.C 113 at [22]. In *Bates v Post Office Ltd (No.2)* [2018] EWHC 2698 (QB), the court refused an application to strike out parts of statements which were made on the basis that the evidence was irrelevant to common issues. It was inappropriate to take too restrictive an approach to relevance in such an application within a group action, given the inherent difficulty of predicting the shape of the case at trial. The evidence would have to be clearly irrelevant for it to be struck out.

[30] See Hodges, *Multi-Party Actions* (2001) (2nd edn by C. Hodges and G. Webb (eds) forthcoming, 2022), pp.15–18. When considering whether to order a preliminary trial of common or generic issues, the objective is to find the best means of dealing with a large number of claims in an expeditious, fair and proportionate way. The court should therefore be cautious about applying to the group litigation context principles which have been developed in ordinary private litigation about the ordering of preliminary issues. See *Varney v Ford Motor Co Ltd* [2013] EWHC 1226 (Ch).

[31] For instance, in the selection of test cases. In general, it will be in the interests of all parties for the test cases to include as many contentious issues as reasonably possible, and to include both strong and weak cases, so that judgment in those test cases will provide the maximum assistance in settling the remaining cases.

[32] In *XYZ v Various Companies* [2013] EWHC 3643 (QB); [2014] Lloyd's Rep. I.R. 431, the court decided, in the context of group litigation relating to medical implants, that it had power to order a defendant to file a witness statement giving details of its ability to fund participation in the group litigation. This would assist the court in managing the case and was therefore a step which could be taken under CPR r.3.1. However, in a subsequent hearing in the same litigation, the court rejected an application by the insurer of one defendant to join the insurer of another defendant. The scope of insurance cover was not an issue connected to the matters in dispute in the proceedings, and so joinder could not be permitted under CPR r.19.2(2). While a general case management power could be exercised flexibly in group litigation, it could not be used to circumvent specific rules: see *XYZ v Various Companies* [2014] EWHC 4056 (QB). See also *Re RBS Rights Issue Litigation* [2017] EWHC 463 (Ch); [2017] 1 W.L.R. 3539, where the court considered applications for disclosure of (i) the names of third-party funders, and (ii) any ATE insurance policy held by the claimants.

[33] In *Saunderson v Sonae Industria (UK) Ltd* [2015] EWHC 2264 (QB) at [456]–[463], the court made critical comments regarding the practices adopted by solicitors in this regard, observing that those adopted (which included leading questionnaires, pop-up shops and cold calling of potential claimants) failed to inspire any degree of confidence.

2. EXPERT EVIDENCE

(a) The Functions of the Expert Witness

Replace paragraph 6-006 (to incorporate new text and footnote and updates to foonotes) with:

In the context of liability issues in professional negligence actions, the expert witness commonly performs two functions.[43] First, the expert sets out and explains the relevant technical matters, e.g. the relevant principles of engineering and how they were applied to the building project in question, or the principles of valuation and how they were applied in the defendant surveyor's valuation or report. To this

6-006

extent, the expert witness is performing a didactic role; explaining the technical aspects of the case in language comprehensible to laymen. Expert evidence of this sort may be largely or wholly uncontroversial. For example, the expert witnesses in a clinical negligence case may agree that the claimant's condition is the result of an adverse reaction to a new drug administered by the defendant. The court must understand and resolve any conflicts between expert evidence of this sort before it can consider the question of negligence. Where there is a dispute on questions of technical fact, the court may prefer the theory advanced by one expert witness over that advanced by another, but it will not assume technical expertise: it will not substitute a theory of its own where that theory is not supported by the evidence of any of the expert witnesses.[44] In principle, a court may reject uncontroverted expert evidence or the common opinion of all the experts on an issue within the relevant scope of expertise. However, if this is to be done, then specific and adequate justification must be given.[44a] The assessment of expert evidence is a matter for the trial judge and an appeal court will be slow to interfere, since the evaluation is likely to be bound up with a wider view of matters of fact. Where the first instance court was a specialist court, such as the Technology and Construction Court, there will be particular caution in reviewing assessment of expert evidence on appeal.[45]

[43] For a general overview and introduction to expert evidence, see P. Coulson (Coulson LJ), I.R. Scott, B. Fontaine (Master Fontaine), J. Sorabji and others (eds) *White Book 2022* (London: Sweet & Maxwell, 2022), Vol.1, Section A, Pt 35; Sir Martin Moore-Bick, P.K.J. Thompson and others (eds), *The Civil Court Practice* (LexisNexis, 2022), Vol.1, Pt 35; S. Sime and D. French (eds), *Blackstone's Civil Practice 2022.*; H. Malek and others (eds), *Phipson on Evidence*, 20th edn (London: Sweet & Maxwell, 2021), Ch.33; C. Hollander, *Documentary Evidence*, 14th edn (London: Sweet & Maxwell, 2021), Ch.31; M. Simpson and others (eds), *Professional Negligence and Liability* Issue 40 (London: Informa, 2022), Ch.24; and M. James, *Expert Evidence: Law and Practice*, 5th edn (London: Sweet & Maxwell, 2020).

[44] In the clinical negligence case *McLean v Weir* (1977) 3 C.C.L.T. 87 in the British Columbia Sup. Ct, Gould J summarised the position in a manner which, it is submitted, is equally applicable in England (at 101):

> "It is true that the court may accept in whole or in part or reject in whole or in part the evidence of any witness on the respective grounds of credibility or plausibility, or a combination of both. But in technical matters, unlike in lay matters within the traditional intellectual competence of the court, it cannot substitute its own medical opinion for that of qualified experts. The court has no status whatsoever to come to a medical conclusion contrary to unanimous medical evidence before it even if it wanted to, which is not the situation in this case. If the medical evidence is equivocal, the court may elect which of the theories advanced it accepts. If only two medical theories are advanced, the court may elect between the two or reject them both; it cannot adopt a third theory of its own, no matter how plausible such might be to the court."

There are some categories of case where the court can more readily take a middle position between experts, or adopt its own approach after considering expert evidence. In the valuers' negligence case of *Capita Alternative Fund Services (Guernsey) Ltd v Drivers Jonas (A Firm)* [2012] EWCA Civ 1417; [2013] 1 E.G.L.R. 119, Gross LJ said (at [43]):

> "It is as well to emphasise that a Judge is never bound by expert evidence (even, though that does not arise here, undisputed expert evidence). While a Judge must have a reasoned or rational basis for a decision—on issues of quantum as on other issues—the Judge is in no way confined to the figures contended for by the experts. This is manifestly so in a typical valuation case where the figure arrived at by the Judge may well lie somewhere in between those advanced by the rival experts. Moreover, having regard to the true nature of quantum disputes and their history as jury questions, a Judge will sometimes find himself needing to do the best he can".

[44a] See *Al-Jedda v Secretary of State for the Home Department* [2012] EWCA Civ 358 at [102]–[107]; *Perkins v McIver* [2012] EWCA Civ 735 at [27]–[31]. For example, in *Maitland-Hudson v Solicitors*

Regulation Authority [2019] EWHC 67 (Admin); [2019] A.C.D. 47 at [82]–[86], the Divisional Court held that the Solicitors Disciplinary Tribunal was not bound by the views of the parties' psychiatric experts in deciding on the appellant's ability to participate in proceedings.

In *Griffiths v TUI Ltd* [2021] EWCA Civ 1442; [2022] 1 W.L.R. 973, it was held on a second appeal that the first instance judge had been entitled to reject the evidence of the sole expert on an issue, even though the evidence was uncontroverted and had been given in writing (with no application to cross-examine). This was a legitimate course on the facts of the case because the expert's evidence was pure assertion, without supporting reasoning

[45] *Wheeldon Bros Waste Ltd v Millennium Insurance Co Ltd* [2018] EWCA Civ 2403; [2019] 4 W.L.R. 56 at [11]–[18].

Replace footnote 49 with:

[49] *DN v Greenwich LBC* [2004] EWCA Civ 1659; [2005] 1 F.C.R. 112. For an example, see *Multiplex Constructions (UK) Ltd v Cleveland Bridge UK Ltd* [2008] EWHC 2220 (TCC), where Jackson J held that in construction litigation an engineer who is giving factual evidence may also proffer (a) statements of opinion which are reasonably related to the facts within his knowledge and (b) relevant comments based on his own expertise. See also *Kirkham v Euro Exide Corp* [2007] EWCA Civ 66; [2007] C.P. Rep. 19 at [16]–[20], where Smith LJ said that a professional witness of fact may give evidence as to what he would have advised in given circumstances, without permission for expert evidence being required. In *Mad Atelier International BV v Manes* [2021] EWHC 1899 (Comm); [2021] 1 W.L.R. 5294, the court confirmed that witnesses of fact may give opinion evidence directly relating to the factual evidence they give, especially in relation to hypothetical and counterfactual questions. Procedural reforms governing witness statements of fact did not alter that legal position on the admissibility of such opinion evidence. See also *Lifestyle Equities CV v Royal County of Berkshire Polo Club Ltd* [2022] EWHC 1244 (Ch), where the court confirmed that witnesses of fact were entitled to give opinion evidence on matters within their experience of a trade.

6-007

(b) Cases Where Expert Evidence is not Required

Replace paragraph 6-011 (to incorporate new text and footnote) with:

In *Michael Hyde & Associates Ltd v JD Williams & Co Ltd*,[68] also an architect's negligence case, the Court of Appeal held that the trial judge had been entitled to conclude that, on the facts of that case, the exercise of judgment involved in deciding whether the defendant was negligent did not of itself require any special architectural skills. The trial judge had not had to "get under the skin of a different profession" in order to assess whether or not the defendants had failed to use reasonable skill and care and, accordingly, had been entitled to make a finding of negligence in spite of expert evidence which supported the defendant's conduct.[69] A detailed discussion of the role of expert evidence in professional negligence claims, particularly claims against construction professionals, is contained in the judgment of Judge Lloyd QC in *Royal Brompton Hospital NHS Trust v Hammond (No.9)*.[70] The judge commented that expert evidence may be needed to assist the court to assess the evidence, for example, by indicating which factors or technical considerations would influence the judgment of a professional person, in cases where the negligence alleged is not a failure to follow an established professional practice. Otherwise, in such cases, expert evidence is not indispensable. The issue of breach of duty may be determined as a matter of common sense. Alternatively, the court may itself possess the necessary expertise to assess the evidence; the Technology and Construction Court has such expertise in disputes arising in the construction industry and in other areas of commerce. Even so, expert evidence may remain desirable in order to satisfy the court that its decision on the required standard of care is in line with the expectations and understanding of the profession. The judge also pointed out that, since the role of the expert witness under the Civil Procedure Rules is to assist the court rather than to make a case for the expert's

6-011

instructing party, it is not necessary for a party which alleges negligence to adduce supporting expert evidence, provided that in a case where such evidence is necessary or desirable it is available from an expert called by another party. Since that case was decided, several further decisions have addressed the need for a party alleging professional negligence to have obtained supportive expert evidence. In *Pantelli Associates Ltd v Corporate City Developments Number Two Ltd*,[71] Coulson J advanced the general proposition that expert evidence ought to be available to a party before an allegation of professional negligence can be put forward, save in one of the exceptional cases identified above.[72] In the subsequent case of *ACD (Landscape Architects) Ltd v Overall*,[73] Akenhead J said that *Pantelli* had laid down no immutable rule of practice that a party may not allege professional negligence in a pleading without having secured supportive expert evidence. He recognised that, even in a case where an allegation of that character may only be made good with expert evidence, there may be good reason for it not to be available when a statement of case is drafted. Similarly, in *Crest Nicholson Operations Ltd v Grafik Architects Ltd*,[73a] the court refused to strike out a professional negligence claim relating to cladding of buildings since the claimant had obtained expert advice when pleading the claim and intended to serve expert evidence in due course.

[68] [2001] P.N.L.R. 8.

[69] [2001] P.N.L.R. 8 at [27]. Ward LJ also observed (at [26]) that the judge would also have been entitled to conclude that the case fell into the second category:

"He may well have been able to discount the evidence on that basis for I find little to suggest that there were two recognised but contrary views of an accepted practice governing the decision in question. As I read the evidence the experts were doing no more than putting themselves forward as reasonably competent architects and then saying what they would have done in the circumstances in which Mr Warrington found himself."

[70] [2002] EWHC 2037 (TCC); 88 Con. L.R. 1 at [16]–[24].

[71] [2010] EWHC 3189 (TCC); [2011] P.N.L.R. 12 at [16]–[19].

[72] This proposition was acknowledged by Akenhead J in *Whessoe Oil & Gas Ltd v Dale* [2012] EWHC 1788 (TCC); [2012] P.N.L.R. 33, but the judge there explained that it was limited in its application to claims for breach of duties by professionals to whose work the *Bolam* test might be applied. It did not extend to a claim against a managing director for breach of contractual duties owed under a business agreement.

[73] [2012] EWHC 100 (TCC); [2012] P.N.L.R. 19 at [16].

[73a] [2021] EWHC 2948 (TCC).

(c)   The Civil Procedure Rules

Replace paragraph 6-012 (to incorporate updates to footnotes 80 and 81) with:

6-012   Lord Woolf's final report on the civil justice system, published in July 1996,[74] heralded a new and restrictive approach to expert evidence which has been embodied in England and Wales in Pt 35 of the Civil Procedure Rules. Under CPR r.35.4, no party may call an expert witness without the court's permission.[75] The principle which guides the court in deciding whether or not to permit expert evidence is set out in CPR r.35.1: expert evidence is to be "restricted to that which is reasonably required to resolve the proceedings."[76] Thus the use of expert evidence is now wholly subject to the control of the court[77] and the court is encouraged to exercise its powers to decide that no expert evidence shall be called upon a particular issue, that a single expert shall be jointly instructed by the parties[78] or that expert evidence should be adduced in writing only.[79] When permission is given for expert evidence, directions will usually provide for simultaneous or sequential exchange of reports and for experts in like disciplines to confer and produce a joint memorandum of points agreed and points disputed.[80] In general, permission is required for expert evidence in all forms of hearing, including interlocutory and final hearings.[81] The court will exercise careful control over both the admission and scope of expert evidence. For example, in the solicitors' negligence case of *Mann v Chetty & Patel*,[82] the Court of Appeal held that expert evidence would be permitted on only one of the quantum issues which arose in the case, whereas the claimant sought to adduce expert evidence on three such issues. The Court of Appeal stated that, in deciding whether to allow expert evidence, the court had to make a judgment on at least three matters:

1. how cogent the proposed expert evidence would be ("cogency");
2. how helpful that evidence would be in resolving any of the issues in the case ("usefulness"); and
3. how much the evidence would cost and the relationship between that cost and the sums at stake ("proportionality").

[74] *Access to Justice* (HMSO, 1996).

[75] This provision concerns permission to adduce the evidence of a witness. Similar permission is not required to rely upon technical literature, although of course the court may be unable to interpret or place reliance on such literature without relevant expert evidence on the subject: *Interflora Inc v Marks and Spencer Plc* [2013] EWHC 936 (Ch) at [14]–[20].

[76] In *Gumpo v Church of Scientology Religious Education College Inc* [2000] C.P. Rep. 38, Smedley J described the policy underlying r.35.1 as being to reduce "the incidence of inappropriate use of experts to bolster cases". Decisions as to the scope of expert evidence which is reasonably required to resolve relevant issues are matters of case management and will accordingly be difficult to disturb on appeal: *Blair-Ford v CRS Adventures Ltd* [2012] EWHC 1886 (QB). However, such decisions must be made in accordance with the overriding objective, and can be challenged where the court has been over-zealous in excluding potentially valuable evidence in the interests of saving costs: *British Airways Plc v Spencer* [2015] EWHC 2477 (Ch); [2015] Pens. L.R. 519 at [19]. *Evans v Frimley Park Hospital NHS Trust* [2012] EWHC 4400 (QB), provides an instance where a defendant made a successful application to adduce additional expert evidence. The court found that an additional haematologist's report which supported the defendant's reasoning "was likely to radically affect the outcome of a trial or have an impact on potential negotiations", and therefore granted the application. See also *Weller v Royal Cornwall Hospital NHS Trust* [2021] EWHC 2332 (QB), where the court permitted the introduction of an expert discipline on the basis that an existing expert had indicated that evidence from the further discipline was required to resolve issues of causation.

[77] The court can be expected to exclude opinion evidence which is "dressed up" as evidence of fact, as for example in *JD Wetherspoon Plc v Harris* [2013] EWHC 1088 (Ch); [2013] 1 W.L.R. 3296 and *Buckingham Homes Ltd v Rutter* [2018] EWHC 3917 (Ch). The requirement for permission for expert evidence cannot be circumvented by annexing to a factual witness statement a document which is intended to provide opinion evidence: see *New Media Distribution Company Sezc Ltd v Kagalovsky* [2018] EWHC 2742 (Ch). However, not every document which contains opinion evidence is governed by Pt 35. In *Rogers v Hoyle* [2014] EWCA Civ 257; [2015] Q.B. 265, the Court of Appeal held that an Air Accident Investigation Branch report was admissible in a negligence action against a pilot who had crashed an aircraft. The narrative portions of the report were admissible as factual evidence and the opinion sections as expert evidence. In admitting the report, the Court of Appeal rejected the submission that the opinion sections had to be admitted under CPR Pt 35 and subject to its provisions. The report was not within the scope of Pt 35; it was admissible documentary evidence, but the court had a discretion under CPR r.32.1 to exclude it if justice and proportionality so dictated. The Court of Appeal drew a distinction with quasi-judicial reports, the factual findings of which are generally inadmissible. This is a significant case and it may be applied directly or by analogy in relation to other forms of report in negligence actions. The principles in *Rogers* were applied in *Mondial Assistance (UK) Ltd v Bridgewater Properties Ltd* [2016] EWHC 3494 (Ch), a landlord and tenant case in which valuation reports adduced by court order attached reports of various technical consultants that had not been obtained for the proceedings. On appeal, Nugee J held that it had been wrong to exclude those technical reports. They were relevant hearsay evidence and not governed by Pt 35. Their content, both factual

and opinion, was admissible. Similarly, in *Illumina Inc. v TDL Genetics Ltd* [2019] EWHC 1159 (Pat), Henry Carr J held that CPR Pt 35 did not apply to hearsay evidence attesting to evidence given by experts in previous proceedings. However, he recognised that the court could exclude such evidence under r.32.1 if the evidence was duplicative or would result in disproportionate costs being incurred.

78 See paras 6-032 to 6-035.

79 CPR r.35.5(1) provides that expert evidence should be given in a written report unless the court directs otherwise. In fast-track cases (those worth between £10,000 and £25,000) experts will not be permitted to give oral evidence unless that is necessary in the interests of justice: CPR r.35.5(2). However, it should be recognised that a judge who attempts to decide between competing expert opinions is faced with a very difficult task unless the experts are called to give oral evidence, a common sense proposition acknowledged in *Preece v Edwards* [2012] EWCA Civ 902 and in *Rengasamy v Homebase Ltd* [2015] EWHC 618 (QB).

80 Failure to comply with the directions of the court may have the result that the defaulting party is not permitted to adduce the relevant expert evidence. Furthermore, a failure by a party and/or its expert to engage properly with the process of expert discussions may cause the court to withdraw permission or impose strict terms to ensure that the process is properly followed: *Mayr v CMS Cameron McKenna Nabarro Olswang LLP* [2018] EWHC 3669 (Comm). In particular, lawyers for a party should not make comments to that party's expert on drafts of the joint memorandum and they should not influence the drafting of such a document save in exceptional circumstances: see *BDW Trading Ltd v Integral Geotechnique (Wales) Ltd* [2018] EWHC 1915 (TCC); [2018] P.N.L.R. 34 at [18]; *Dana UK Axle Ltd v Freudenberg FST GmbH* [2021] EWHC 1413 (TCC); [2021] B.L.R. 500 at [66]–[87]; *Andrews v Kronospan Ltd* [2022] EWHC 479 (QB) at [16]–[25]. A joint memorandum of experts is a document for the assistance of the court. In *Aderonmu v Colvin* [2021] EWHC 2293 (QB), the memoranda were criticised as being over-long, "lawyered" documents filled with cross-examination questions on both sides. The court commented that a joint memorandum "should not be a proving ground for the parties' respective cases".

81 See for example *B.B. Energy (Gulf) DMCC v Al Amoudi* [2018] EWHC 2595 (Comm) at [49], where an attempt to rely upon expert evidence of foreign law as an annex to a solicitor's statement in a jurisdictional dispute was rejected. Note, however, that in a security for costs application or freezing order application, a more flexible approach is taken and it is not generally necessary to comply with all the requirements of CPR Pt 35: *Pipia v Bgeo Group Ltd* [2019] EWHC 325 (Comm) (citing *Bestfort Developments LLP v Ras Al Khaimah Investment Authority* [2016] EWCA Civ 1099; [2017] C.P. Rep. 9). In a summary judgment application, an expert report may in principle be considered, although no permission for its use has been granted, in support of the proposition that a party can expect to rely upon particular expert views: see *Ross v Attanta* [2021] EWHC 503 (Comm); [2021] P.N.L.R. 18 at [6]. However, an attempt to rely upon expert evidence for broader purposes without permission was refused in *Tchenguiz v IG Index Ltd* [2022] EWHC 793 (Ch).

82 [2001] Lloyd's Rep. P.N. 38 CA. See also the accountants' negligence case of *Barings Plc (In Liquidation) v Coopers & Lybrand* [2001] Lloyd's Rep. P.N. 379.

In paragraph 6-013, after "to be resolved.", add:

6-013   By contrast, on issues of foreign law, there is no universal rule that the content of another state's law needs to be proved by an expert witness, and that may be done in appropriate cases by reference to case law and authoritative text books.[91a]

91a See *Brownlie v FS Cairo (Nile Plaza) LLC* [2021] UKSC 45; [2021] 3 W.L.R. 1011 at [148]–[149], per Lord Leggatt JSC. This point of practice is reflected in section H3 of the Commercial Court Guide (11th edn). In *Suppipat v Narongdej* [2022] EWHC 1806 (Comm), it was decided that Singapore law (which shared common law roots with English law) should be given not by an expert but by reference to sources.

After "Court, Chancery Division),", add new footnote 94a:

6-015   94a See also the speech of Lord Hamblen JSC to the Expert Witness Online Conference 2022 (at *https ://www.supremecourt.uk/docs/ewi-speech-may-22.pdf* [Accessed 30 September 2022]) which provides practical guidance to lawyers and experts on their dealings with each other and the court in modern civil litigation.

Replace footnote 110 with:

6-018   110 See also *Fetaj v Cohen* [2019] EWHC 2803 (Ch), where the claimants attempted to change experts on the basis that theirs had been subjected to undue pressure in an experts' meeting. The court rejected the attempt, stressing that such an allegation would have to be made clearly and the experts given an opportunity to respond. Similarly, in *Fernandez v Iceland Foods Ltd* [2021] EWHC 3723 (QB), the court refused to permit a party to adduce evidence of a new expert in substitution for that of an expert whose opinion had changed. There was good reason for the change of mind, and expert-shopping should not be allowed.

(d)   Relevance and Admissibility of Expert Evidence

(ii)   The Appropriate Questions

Replace footnote 131 with:

[131] In *Dana UK Axle Ltd v Freudenberg FST GmbH* [2021] EWHC 1413 (TCC); [2021] B.L.R. 500, the court excluded evidence from the defendant's experts on the basis that they had been provided with information and guidance from its in-house technical specialists without the claimant being informed.   **6-024**

(iii)   The Appropriate Qualifications and Experience

Replace footnote 135 with:

[135] See also the *Commercial Court Guide*, 11th edn, Appendix 8: an expert should state the assumptions upon which his opinion is based, and if a stated assumption is, in the opinion of the expert, unreasonable or unlikely, he should state that clearly.   **6-025**

(iv)   Impartiality

In paragraph 6-030, after "which is anyway", replace "specifically prohibited by para.7.6 of the Protocol for the Instruction of Experts." with:

strongly discouraged by para.88 of the Guidance for Instruction of Experts In Civil Claims.   **6-030**

(f)   Experts' Immunity from Suit

After paragraph 6-038, add new paragraph:

Since the decision in *Jones*, there have been relatively few reported cases of claims against expert witnesses. One important example is the case of *Radia v Marks*,[187a] where a claimant sued a medical expert who had acted as a single joint expert in employment tribunal proceedings. The claimant claimed that the mis-reporting of his account in a consultation had led to him being disbelieved by the tribunal, losing his claim and incurring a costs liability. It was common ground that the expert owed the claimant a duty in assessing and reporting on his condition. However, it was held that the scope of the duty did not extend to protecting the claimant from an adverse finding on credibility, not least because that would create a conflict between the expert's duties to the client and the court which, on the analysis in *Jones*, were not in conflict. The claim also failed on other grounds, notably causation.   **6-038A**

[187a] [2022] EWHC 145 (QB); [2022] P.N.L.R. 12.

CHAPTER 7

HUMAN RIGHTS AND JUDICIAL REVIEW IN PROFESSIONAL
LIABILITY

1. INTRODUCTION

Replace footnote 1 with:

7-001   [1] For example see A. Patrick and others (eds), *Human Rights Practice*, Rel.43 (London: Sweet & Maxwell, 2022); D. Harris and others (eds), *Harris, O'Boyle and Warbrick: Law of the European Convention on Human Rights*, 4th edn (Oxford: Oxford University Press, 2018); K. Reid, *A Practitioner's Guide to the European Convention on Human Rights*, 6th edn (London: Sweet & Maxwell, 2019) (7th edn, forthcoming, 2023); Lord Lester, Lord Pannick, J. Herberg and others (eds), *Human Rights Law and Practice*, 3rd edn (London: LexisNexis, 2009) (4th edn, forthcoming, 2022); and R. Clayton, H. Tomlinson and others (eds), *The Law of Human Rights*, 2nd edn (Oxford: Oxford University Press, 2009). See too, W.A. Schabas, *The European Convention on Human Rights: A Commentary* (Oxford: Oxford University Press, 2015) and Sir Jack Beatson, S. Grosz, T. Hickman, R. Singh and S. Palmer, *Human Rights: Judicial Protection in the United Kingdom* (London: Sweet & Maxwell, 2008).

5. LAWYERS

(b)   Lawyer/Client Confidentiality and the Convention

In paragraph 7-046, after "by prison authorities.", add new footnote 117a:

7-046   [117a] For a domestic application of the relevant principles in that specific context see the decision of Heather Williams J in *R. (on the application of Xavier) v Governor of Whitemoor Prison* [2021] EWHC 3060 (Admin).

(c)   Freedom of Expression/Association

Replace paragraph 7-058 (to incorporate footnote updates and new text and footnotes) with:

7-058   In *Kyprianou v Cyprus*,[145] the European Court found a violation of art.10 in circumstances where a lawyer was found guilty of contempt and sentenced to five days' imprisonment following his objection to a judicial remark regarding the manner of his cross-examination which he found offensive and his refusal to proceed with the cross-examination. The court stated that the imposition of a disproportionately severe and immediate sentence of imprisonment where a lawyer, acting in the best interests of his client, objected or complained about the conduct of the court would result in lawyers feeling constrained in making such representations and have a chilling effect on the profession as a whole.[146] In *Attorney General v Crossland*,[146a] the Attorney General brought contempt of court proceedings against an unregistered barrister who had disclosed the outcome of a judgment of the Supreme Court which was still in draft and subject to embargo. The imposition of an embargo prior to hand down of a judgment is an interference with art.10 and accordingly, to be punishable, it must be justified. In referring to *Kyprianou v Cyprus*[146b] Lady Arden (dissenting, albeit on a different point) held that it was not just the penalty for contempt but the conviction for it that had to be justified. On the facts, the finding of contempt was a lawful interference with the defendant's art.10 rights: he knew that disclosure was prohibited, and was a contempt, and had intended to interfere with the due administration of justice notwithstanding his motive of securing what he believed to be a just outcome overall.

[145] (73797/01) 15 December 2005; (2007) 44 E.H.R.R. 27; [2006] 2 E.H.R.L.R. 220.

[146] See also *Foglia v Switzerland* (35865/04) 13 March 2008, where the European Court found a breach of art.10 where a lawyer had been disciplined with a fine for alleged unprofessional conduct in giving comments and access to trial documents to the press and *Veraart v Netherlands* (2008) 46 E.H.R.R. 53 where the European Court found a breach of art.10 where a lawyer had been disciplined for making a public statement outside the courtroom but the tribunal had not made an adequate assessment of the relevant facts such as to enable it to give an informed decision as to whether the lawyer had overstepped the limits of acceptable professional behaviour. See also *Matalas v Greece* (2021) 73 E.H.R.R. 26 where a criminal conviction, which resulted from proceedings initiated by a legal advisor for slanderous defamation, was not justified when balancing the applicant's art.10 rights against the legal advisor's right to a reputation under art.8.

[146a] [2021] UKSC 58; [2022] 1 W.L.R 367.

[146b] (73797/01) 15 December 2005; (2007) 44 E.H.R.R. 27; [2006] 2 E.H.R.L.R. 220.

Replace paragraph 7-060 (to incorporate new text and footnotes) with:

In *Morice v France*,[151] the applicant, a lawyer, sent a letter of complaint concern- **7-060** ing the conduct of a judge to the Minister of Justice, asking for an investigation into the judge's behaviour. Extracts from the letter and statements made by the applicant about the judge were published in a newspaper article. A criminal complaint of defamation was filed against the applicant, he was committed to stand trial, and ultimately found guilty of complicity in public defamation. The European Court of Human Rights held the applicant's criminal conviction constituted an interference with the exercise of his right to freedom of expression under art.10. The applicant's remarks were aimed at investigating judges who had been removed from the proceedings and did not directly contribute to the applicant's task of defending his client. His remarks fell within a debate on a matter of public interest and called for a high level of protection of freedom of expression. By contrast, in the domestic context, in *Kwiatkowski v Bar Standards Board*,[151a] a barrister made inappropriate and sexist comments in the public waiting area of a county court to a female barrister about why women were unsuited to the legal profession. In disciplinary proceedings the BSB found that the behaviour had diminished the trust and confidence that the public placed in barristers and the profession. On appeal, it was argued that, contrary to the appellant's art.10 rights, the effect of the BSB's decision was to prevent a barrister from expressing opinions which some of the population deemed to be unacceptable. In dismissing the appeal, Choudhury J held that the BSB tribunal had properly evaluated the art.10 considerations, both in terms of necessity and proportionality, and that barristers were expected not to conduct themselves in a discriminatory manner and not to use language that is clearly sexist and discriminatory in a professional setting in a public place. The underlying rationale was not to curb barristers from holding views that some might find deplorable. Rather "it is the public confidence in barristers and the profession that requires protection". Further, "[t]he fact that an individual barrister might not object to engaging in debate with colleagues espousing offensive and discriminatory views does not diminish the erosion of public confidence that is likely to result from such conduct".[151b]

[151] (2016) 62 E.H.R.R. 1.

[151a] [2022] EWHC 1800 (Admin).

[151b] [2022] EWHC 1800 (Admin) at [77].

7. PARTICULAR ISSUES ARISING UNDER THE HRA IN RELATION TO MEDICAL PRACTITIONERS

(a) Clinical Negligence and the Bolam Test

Replace paragraph 7-077 (to incorporate updates to footnotes 267 and 268) with:

7-077 Prior to the coming into force of the Act, it had been suggested by some practitioners that art.2 might provide a means for challenging the long established *Bolam* test and the court's adherence to the "respectable body of medical opinion" approach.[267] The argument put forward was that the *Bolam* test is inconsistent with the right to life unless the domestic courts construe the requirement to take reasonable care as equivalent to the requirement to make adequate provision for medical care. If the care provided is negligent then, by definition, it will not have been adequate. However, the converse may not apply and care that is inadequate is not necessarily negligent. Despite such anticipation, such a challenge is yet to be successfully mounted. Nevertheless, the potential for using the Human Rights Act in clinical negligence cases to challenge the *Bolam* test continues to be advocated at an academic level.[268]

[267] See further, S. Pattinson, *Medical Law and Ethics*, 6th edn (London: Sweet & Maxwell, 2020) and J. Herring, *Medical Law and Ethics*, 9th edn (Oxford: Oxford University Press, 2022). For comprehensive coverage of this area see the following specialist work: D. Gomez and others (eds), *The Regulation of Healthcare Professionals: Law, Principle and Process*, 2nd edn (London: Sweet & Maxwell, 2019).

[268] See M. Simpson and others (eds), *Professional Negligence and Liability*, Issue 40 (London: Informa Law, 2022), Ch.14 section viii "Clinical Practitioners: The Impact of the Human Rights Act 1998".

(c) Withdrawal of Treatment

In paragraph 7-084, after "of medical treatment:", add new footnote 286a:

7-084 [286a] See also the decision of the Fourth Section of the ECtHR in *Parfitt v UK* (App. no.18533/21) (2021) 73 E.H.R.R. SE1, applying the principles set out in *Gard v UK (Admissibility)* to a case of withdrawal of treatment from a six-year-old child. The application was brought on, inter alia, art.2 and art.8 grounds, and was ruled inadmissible: [45] and [53].

Replace footnote 292 with:

7-088 [292] For subsequent restatements of this principle, see the Court of Appeal's judgments in *Re Knight (A Child)* [2021] EWCA Civ 362; [2021] Med. L.R. 323 and *Fixsler v Manchester University NHS Foundation Trust* [2021] EWCA Civ 1018; [2021] 4 W.L.R. 123. The principles in *Aintree* were applied in *Barts Health NHS Trust v Dance* [2022] EWFC 80. Permission to appeal on, inter alia, human rights grounds was refused by the Court of Appeal (see [2022] EWCA Civ 1055, [26]).

Replace paragraph 7-093 (to incorporate new text and footnotes) with:

7-093 In *Gloucestershire Clinical Commissioning Group v (1) AB (2) CD*,[302] Baker J reiterated that in making a decision concerning life sustaining treatment, the court must have regard to the ECHR, and in particular arts 2 and 8. Article 2 imposed a positive obligation to give life sustaining treatment if this was in the best interests of the patient but did not impose an absolute obligation to treat if treatment was futile. Article 8 encompassed considerations of a patient's personal autonomy and quality of life. In *Re A (A Child) (Withdrawal of Treatment: Legal Representation)*[302a] the parents in a withdrawal of treatment case sought an adjournment of the hearing of the substantive application in order that they could obtain legal representation. Hayden J refused, and the parents appealed on procedural unfairness grounds, both at common law and relying on art.6. The Court of Appeal upheld the appeal, finding the refusal of the adjournment procedurally unfair given the grave importance of the matters at stake, the importance of the parents having legal representation, and the fact that they had lost their previous representation at short notice through no fault of their own. The court considered the refusal unfair as a matter of common law but held that it was unnecessary to consider whether it breached art.6 as well "because the Human Rights Act 1998 should not normally be treated as the starting point in any case in which human rights issues arise given the protection of human rights under the common law or statute".[302b]

[302] [2014] EWCOP 49; (2015) 142 B.M.L.R. 242.

[302a] [2022] EWCA Civ 1221.

[302b] [2022] EWCA Civ 1221 at [27].

(d)　Consent to Treatment

Replace paragraph 7-098 (to incorporate new text and footnote) with:

By contrast in *A NHS Foundation Trust v X*,[309] Cobb J held that arts 3 and 8 were **7-098** particularly prominently engaged in the case of a young woman with a 14-year history of anorexia nervosa. He held that repeated forcible feeding over a long period of time against her clearly expressed wishes, most especially with the use of physical restraint, was likely to amount to inhuman or degrading treatment and would certainly amount to a severe interference with her private life and autonomy. In *Re E (Children: Blood Transfusion)*[309a] two young people, aged 16 and 17, refused to receive blood transfusions on religious grounds. They had capacity to make decisions about their medical treatment and had the support of their parents. The court nonetheless held under its inherent jurisdiction that, as they were minors, it would be lawful for their doctors to administer blood to them in the course of an operation if it became necessary to prevent serious injury or death. The individuals were distressed that their autonomy had been overruled and by the decision-making process. The Court of Appeal upheld the court below, including rejecting claims that the decision breached their art.8 and art.9 ECHR rights.

[309] [2014] EWCOP 35; [2015] C.O.P.L.R. 11.

[309a] [2021] EWCA Civ 1888; [2022] Fam. 130.

8. PROFESSIONAL DISCIPLINARY PROCEEDINGS

(b) Procedural Guarantees

Independence and impartiality

Replace paragraph 7-125 (to incorporate new text and footnote) with:

7-125   In *Aaron v Law Society*[378] the court stated that, in relation to claims of objective bias the test was whether in the circumstances a fair-minded observer would have considered that there had been a real possibility of bias. In *Holder v Law Society*,[379] the Divisional Court held that the Solicitors Disciplinary Tribunal was an independent and impartial tribunal that complied with art.6. It noted that appointments to the tribunal were made by the Master of the Rolls through an open selection process and the Law Society was not involved in those appointments.[380] In *Bibi v Bar Standards Board*[380a] the appellant had been disbarred. About two years prior, she had been convicted of council tax fraud. The appellant argued that the BSB tribunal was biased and had predetermined the case, as it had read the Crown Court's judgment and seen the comments in it about her honesty. Hill J, dismissing the appeal, held that the Tribunal was a skilled and expert body, well able to reach its own conclusions, uninfluenced by those of a different tribunal.

[378] [2003] EWHC 2271 (Admin).

[379] [2005] EWHC 2023 (Admin); [2006] P.N.L.R. 10.

[380] See also *Simms v Law Society* [2005] EWHC 408 (Admin); *Pine v Law Society* [2001] EWCA Civ 1574; [2002] 1 W.L.R. 2189.

[380a] [2022] EWHC 921 (Admin).

Appeals

Replace paragraph 7-157 (to incorporate new text and footnotes) with:

7-157   In cases such as *Hayes v Law Society*[469] the court has applied this approach to appeals from solicitors' disciplinary proceedings, treating the case as a rehearing, albeit one within which the decision-making body is accorded appropriate respect. A similar approach was taken to appeals from osteopaths' disciplinary proceedings in *Moody v General Osteopathic Council*.[470] Time limits for appeals against disciplinary decisions are also to be interpreted consistently with art.6. In *Adesina v Nursing and Midwifery Council*,[471] the Court of Appeal held that the prima facie absolute 28-day time limit for appealing against a disciplinary decision of the Nursing and Midwifery Council was to be read down in a manner compatible with art.6, so as to allow for an extension in exceptional circumstances. However, on the facts, the appellants failed to demonstrate that their cases were exceptional. The adverse decisions were announced in their presence and subsequent delays were largely or entirely the fault of the appellants. In *Parkin v Nursing and Midwifery Council*,[472] Eder J, applying *Adesina*, held that the reading down was limited to the minimum extent necessary to secure ECHR compliance. Extensions of time should therefore only be granted in "very limited" circumstances. Although the notice of appeal was lodged less than a day late, the applicant had instructed solicitors in time to prepare the case, and the reason for the delay was that his solicitors had not been aware of the deadline for lodging, these were not sufficiently exceptional matters to justify an extension of time for lodging the appeal. In *Nursing and Midwifery Council v Daniels*,[473] the Court of Appeal overturned the High Court's extension of time for appealing against a decision of the Nursing and Midwifery Council. It held that in circumstances where the appellant did not contact her lawyers until the last day before the expiry of the 28-day time limit and those lawyers acted expeditiously to file an appellant's notice, there were no exceptional circumstances justifying an extension. Jackson LJ noted that if the court had had a general discretion to extend time, the decision below would have been without fault. However, they did not, and could only do so in exceptional circumstances, which there were not on the facts. In *Rakoczy v General Medical Council*,[473a] an appeal against a decision of the Medical Practitioners Tribunal was not properly filed and so was struck out. Fordham J refused an application to set aside that decision and extend time. The judge held that, although the case law generally describes a "discretion" or "power" to extend time, in cases where the refusal to extend time would result in a breach of art.6— which is "the only situation in which the function of extending time is appropriately exercised"[473b]—it is more correct to speak of a "duty", because not only is the Court empowered to act, but it would be necessary for it to do so. Even on the most favourable interpretation of the authorities to the applicant, of which the judge provided a detailed exposition, this was not a case which demanded that time be extended.

[469] [2004] EWHC 1165 (QB).

[470] [2004] EWHC 967 (Admin).

[471] [2013] EWCA Civ 818; [2013] 1 W.L.R. 3156.

[472] [2014] EWHC 519 (Admin).

[473] [2015] EWCA Civ 225; [2015] Med. L.R. 255.

[473a] [2022] EWHC 890 (Admin).

[473b] [2022] EWHC 890 (Admin) at [22(ix)].

9. JUDICIAL REVIEW CHALLENGES AND PROFESSIONAL LIABILITY

Replace footnote 481 with:

[481] For a comprehensive account of judicial review see: Lord Woolf, Sir Jeffery Jowell, C. Donnelly and I. Hare (eds), *De Smith's Judicial Review*, 8th edn (London: Sweet & Maxwell, 2018; 4th supp, 2021); H. Fenwick, Sir Michael Supperstone, J. Goudie and Sir Paul Walker (eds), *Judicial Review*, 6th edn (London: LexisNexis, 2017; 1st supp, 2019); J. Auburn, J. Moffat and A. Sharland, *Judicial Review: Principles and Procedure* (Oxford: Oxford University Press, 2013); and Sir Michael Fordham, *Judicial Review Handbook*, 7th edn (Hart Publishing, 2020).

7-162

(a) Financial Ombudsman Service

(i) FOS: Substantive challenges

Replace paragraph 7-168 (to incorporate new text and footnote) with:

A decision by the FOS cannot be challenged on the basis that the FOS failed to apply the law. It is now well established that the FOS is entitled to depart from the law.[489] However, in line with the reasoning of Stanley Burton LJ in *R. (on the application of Heather Moor & Edgecomb Ltd) v Financial Ombudsman Service*,[490] any such departure must be explained in the Financial Ombudsman's decision, providing reasons for the departure. A determination may be challenged on the ground that it was inconsistent with the evidence: *R. (on the application of Garrison Investment Analysis) v Financial Ombudsman Service*.[491] However, as with challenges to findings of fact on appeal from a trial, the question is not whether the

7-168

court would have made the finding of fact which the ombudsman did, but whether there was sufficient evidential basis for the finding not to be irrational: *R. (on the application of Green) v Financial Ombudsman Service*.[492] The true construction of contractual documents is a matter for the courts,[493] applying ordinary principles, but whether a party to such a contract has exercised its discretion reasonably under its terms is a matter for the FOS decision-maker.[494] Similarly, the construction of any relevant rules, for instance those found in the FCA Handbook, is a matter for the courts. However, the application of those rules to the facts of the case is a matter for the FOS decision-maker, who will be given "considerable leeway": *R. v Financial Ombudsman Service Ex p Norwich and Peterborough Building Society*[495]; *R. (on the application of Berkeley Burke SIPP Administration Ltd) v Financial Ombudsman Service*.[496] The question is whether the decision was unlawful, not whether it is possible to disagree with the application of the principles to the facts;[496a] a challenge which amounts essentially to a disagreement with the conclusions reached is, it is submitted, highly unlikely to succeed without more. Equally, the weight to be given to any particular evidence in the determination of the facts is "quintessentially a judgment for the decision-maker, and not susceptible to legal challenge in the absence of public law error": *R (on the application of Critchley) v Financial Ombudsman Service Ltd*.[497] A decision of the FOS may be challenged on the ground of inconsistency with another of its decisions. But inconsistencies in outcome across similar areas of complaint, albeit on different facts, may merely serve to confirm that the FOS decision-maker is "considering each case individually, and not applying an unlawful policy or set of counter-presumptions" in the same way that different judges may lawfully reach different conclusions in similar cases, that being a feature of any independent judicial system: *R. (on the application of Critchley) v Financial Ombudsman Service Ltd*.[498] Moreover, inconsistency between a decision of the FOS and that of another body, created by a different statutory scheme, will generally not provide a basis for challenge: *R. (on the application of Berkeley Burke SIPP Administration Ltd) v Financial Ombudsman Service*.[499]

[489] *R. (on the application of IFG Financial Services Ltd) v Financial Ombudsman Service* [2005] EWHC 1153 (Admin); [2006] 1 B.C.L.C. 534. See also *R. (on the application of Aviva Life and Pensions (UK) Ltd) v Financial Ombudsman Service* [2017] EWHC 352 (Admin); [2017] Lloyd's Rep. I.R. 404 and the obiter reservations of Jay J at [73] regarding the nature of the FOS's jurisdiction which "occupies an uncertain space outside the common law and statute".

[490] [2008] EWCA Civ 642; [2008] Bus. L.R. 1486.

[491] [2006] EWHC 2466 (Admin).

[492] [2012] EWHC 1253 (Admin).

[493] See *R. (on the application of TF Global Markets (UK) Ltd) v Financial Ombudsman Service Ltd* [2020] EWHC 3178 (Admin); [2021] A.C.D. 19, where HHJ Karen Walden-Smith (sitting as a judge of the High Court), applying *Wood v Capital Insurance Services Ltd* [2017] UKSC 24; [2017] A.C. 1173 as to the principles engaged in the interpretation of contracts, at [42], held that the FOS decision-maker had erred in his construction of a contract between the parties as he had "failed to read the clause in the context of the entire contract", instead focusing on one particular clause to the exclusion of other, relevant, clauses.

[494] *R. (on the application of TF Global Markets (UK) Ltd) v Financial Ombudsman Service Ltd* [2020] EWHC 3178 (Admin); [2021] A.C.D. 19 at [51], where the matter was remitted to the FOS decision-maker to determine whether a party to the contract had exercised its discretion in accordance with the duty set out in *Braganza v BP Shipping Ltd* [2015] UKSC 17; [2015] 1 W.L.R. 1661, i.e. not arbitrarily, capriciously or unreasonably.

[495] [2002] EWHC 2379 (Admin); [2003] 1 All E.R. (Comm) 65.

[496] [2018] EWHC 2878 (Admin); [2019] Bus. L.R. 437 at [82] and [137].

[496a] See *R. (on the application of Portal Financial Services LLP) v Financial Ombudsman Service Ltd* [2022] EWHC 710 (Admin) at [18]. This was an application for permission for judicial review where Sweeting J, in refusing permission, took the opportunity to reinforce the notion that the Ombudsman system was designed to provide an independent and informal complaint resolution procedure, which operated quickly and with minimal formality without recourse to the courts ([30]).

[497] [2019] EWHC 3036 (Admin); [2020] Lloyd's Rep. I.R. 176 at [91].

[498] [2019] EWHC 3036 (Admin); [2020] Lloyd's Rep. I.R. 176 at [100]–[101], where Lang J declined to find an inconsistency across two FOS decisions relating to payment protection insurance where the facts were "significantly different".

[499] [2018] EWHC 2878 (Admin); [2019] Bus. L.R. 437 at [138]–[145].

Replace paragraph 7-169 (to incorporate new text and footnote) with:

One potentially promising area for challenge by way of judicial review is **7-169** jurisdiction. The issue of whether or not a complaint falls within the FOS's jurisdiction will typically depend on the application of relevant provisions of FSMA and DISP conferring or withholding jurisdiction. Examples have included: whether the complaint was brought within time (*R. (on the application of Bankole) v Financial Ombudsman Service*[500]); whether a complainant was a "consumer" (*R. (on the application of Bluefin Insurance Services Ltd) v Financial Ombudsman Service*[501]); whether or not advice complained about was tax advice or investment advice (*R. (on the application of Chancery (UK) LLP) v Financial Ombudsman Service Ltd*[502]); whether the scheme concerned was a collective investment scheme (ibid.); whether a complaint about a firm's handling of an internal complaint was about the provision or failure to provide a financial service" (*R. (on the application of Mazarona Properties Ltd) v Financial Ombudsman Service*[503]); whether or not advice on both regulated and unregulated investments amounted to "regulated activity" (*R. (on the application of TenetConnect) v Financial Ombudsman*[504]); and whether the FOS had jurisdiction to consider historic interest rates applied to a mortgage, beyond the six-year time limit for bringing a complaint, as part of assessing whether the interest rates applied within the six-year period were fair and reasonable (*R. (on the application of Mortgage Agency Services Number Five Ltd) v Financial Ombudsman Service*[504a]). Although the court will attach weight to the expertise of persons such as the FOS in the context of jurisdictional issues, it is ultimately a matter for the courts to decide the limits of the FOS's jurisdiction. As noted by Ouseley J in *Chancery (UK) LLP* "the FSMA should not be construed so as to make the FOS master of the limits of its jurisdiction, right or wrong. It is for the Court to decide whether it has acted with or without jurisdiction."[505] However, there is a distinction between the legal test for jurisdiction (which is for the court) and the facts to which that legal test is applied (which is for the FOS). In the words of Ouseley J: "Is there a distinction between tax advice and investment advice, and if so, on the facts found by the FOS, was advice given here which was a regulated activity? Both of these aspects are for the Court but on the facts as rationally found by the FOS".[506]

[500] [2012] EWHC 3555 (Admin).

[501] [2014] EWHC 3413 (Admin); [2015] Bus. L.R. 656.

[502] [2015] EWHC 407 (Admin); [2015] B.T.C 13.

[503] [2017] EWHC 1135 (Admin); [2017] A.C.D. 94.

[504] [2018] EWHC 459 (Admin); [2018] 1 B.C.L.C 726.

[504a] [2022] EWHC 1979 (Admin). In that case, Griffiths J held that the FOS did not err in considering interest variations before the six-year period as background, or context, for the complaints within that period. There was nothing Wednesbury unreasonable or unlawful about the decision because, in considering the fairness of the interest charges within the FOS' jurisdiction, it needed to look at the impact (if any) of what may or may not have contributed to those charges, including those that may have happened more than six years from the date of the complaint ([93]).

[505] [2015] EWHC 407 (Admin); [2015] B.T.C 13 at [66].

[506] [2015] EWHC 407 (Admin); [2015] B.T.C 13 at [67].

CHAPTER 8

PROFESSIONAL INDEMNITY INSURANCE

1. INTRODUCTION

Replace footnote 1 with:

8-001   [1] For a general introduction to professional indemnity insurance, see M. Cannon and B. McGurk, *Professional Indemnity Insurance*, 2nd edn (Oxford: Oxford University Press, 2016), Ch.1, see too, W.I.B. Enright and D.C. Jess, *Professional Indemnity Insurance Law*, 2nd edn (London: Sweet & Maxwell, 2007) (3rd edn, forthcoming, 2024).

3. THE NATURE/SCOPE OF PROFESSIONAL INDEMNITY INSURANCE

Replace footnote 51 with:

8-019   [51] It is not enough that the liability should be related to the insured's business. Thus, by way of example, a liability pursuant to an undertaking given by a solicitor in relation to a transaction on which he was not involved has been found to fall outside the scope of his professional indemnity cover: *Halliwells LLP v NES Solicitors* [2011] EWHC 947 (QB); [2011] P.N.L.R. 30. So also the liability of a firm of solicitors as guarantors for its clients' obligations in respect of loans advanced to fund the payment of disbursements in litigation: *Sutherland Professional Funding Ltd v Bakewells (A Firm)* [2011] EWHC 2658 (QB); [2013] Lloyd's Rep. I.R. 93. And the liability of a solicitors' practice for breach of trust arising from an agreement with its providers of commercial finance: *Doorway Capital Ltd v American International Group UK Ltd* [2022] EWHC 182 (Comm), Butcher J. See the description of professional indemnity insurance in *Impact Funding Solutions Ltd v Barrington Support Services Ltd* [2016] UKSC 57; [2017] A.C. 73 at [42] per Lord Toulson.

9. RULES OF CONSTRUCTION

(b) Exclusion Clauses and Insuring Clauses

Replace footnote 190 with:

8-065   [190] [2016] UKSC 57; [2017] A.C. 73 at [35]. See also [32] per Lord Hodge. This approach was followed in *Crowden v QBE Insurance (Europe) Ltd* [2017] EWHC 2597 (Comm); [2018] Lloyd's Rep.

I.R. 83, in which Peter MacDonald Eggers QC held that an "insolvency" exclusion commonly found in professional indemnity policies for independent financial advisers was effective to exclude liabilities even though the FSA handbook required IFAs to maintain insurance in respect of the self-same liabilities: as the deputy judge observed at [85], it was incumbent on the insured, not insurers, to ensure that the insured obtained sufficient professional indemnity cover. It was also followed in *Doorway Capital Ltd v American International Group UK Ltd* [2022] EWCA 182 (Comm), in which Butcher J held that even if a claim for breach of trust against the solicitor by its provider of commercial finance was covered by the main insuring clause (which he held it was not), it nonetheless fell within an exclusion in respect of liability "under any contract or agreement for the supply to, or use by, the Insured of goods or services in the course of the Insured Firm's Practice".

16. DEDUCTIBLES AND LIMITS OF INDEMNITY; AGGREGATION OF CLAIMS

(a) Generally

Replace paragraph 8-133 (to incorporate new text and footnotes) with:

Perhaps counter-intuitively, "cause", "original cause" and "originating cause" **8-133** connote a wider relationship than "event". In *Axa Reinsurance (UK) Plc v Field*, the House of Lords held that use of the word "originating" was intended to "open up the widest possible search for a unifying factor".[336] In *Spire Healthcare Ltd v Royal and Sun Alliance Ltd* the Court of Appeal held that the misconduct of a single, serially negligent and dishonest consultant was the "one source or original cause" to which 750 claims by former patients were attributable, even though the pattern of incompetence manifested itself in different ways.[336a] However, the phrase "original cause" is not to be construed at such a level of abstraction as to render the requirement for a real causal link illusory.[337] Not every "but for" cause is sufficient to amount to an "original cause".[338]

[336] [1996] 1 W.L.R. 1026 at 1035. See also *Countrywide Assured Group Plc v DJ Marshall* [2002] EWHC 2082 (Comm); [2003] Lloyd's Rep. I.R. 195.

[336a] [2022] EWCA Civ 17; [2022] P.N.L.R. 15.

[337] See *American Centennial Insurance Co v INSCO Ltd* [1996] L.R.I.R. 407 at 414 (col.1) per Moore-Bick J; *The Cultural Foundation (t/a American School of Dubai) v Beazley Furlonge Ltd* [2018] EWHC 1083 (Comm); [2019] Lloyd's Rep. I.R. 12 at [204(iii)] per Andrew Henshaw QC.

[338] *Spire Healthcare Ltd v Royal and Sun Alliance Ltd* [2022] EWCA Civ 17; [2022] P.N.L.R. 15, per Andrews LJ at [24].

CHAPTER 9

CONSTRUCTION PROFESSIONALS

TABLE OF CONTENTS

[53]

1. INTRODUCTION

(a) The Construction Professionals

In paragraph 9-001, after "a building contractor.", add new footnote 0:

9-001   ⁰ The categories of construction professional are not closed. New and more sophisticated construction contracts and new and more sophisticated construction techniques have led to new forms of professional arising out of old forms (for example, project managers emerging as a distinct profession largely from the ranks of quantity surveyors). Persons involved in construction projects in a professional capacity may be engaged in a wide variety of consultancy. One example is Approved Inspectors—renamed as Building Control Approvers—whose purely statutory functions are not consultancy at all (see *Lessees and Management Company of Herons Court v Heronslea Ltd* [2019] EWCA Civ 1423; [2019] 1 W.L.R. 5849), but who may additionally offer consultancy on a contractual basis.

(c) The Construction Industry

Replace footnote 22 with:

9-013   ²² For example see N. Dennys and R. Clay, *Hudson's Building and Engineering Contracts*, 14th edn (London: Sweet & Maxwell, 2020, 1st supp, 2021); S. Furst, Sir Vivian Ramsey and others (eds), *Keating on Construction Contracts*, 11th edn (London: Sweet & Maxwell, 2021, 1st supp, 2021); Crown Office Chambers, *Emden's Construction Law*, Issue 215 (London: LexisNexis, 2022).

2. DUTIES

(a) Duties to Client

(ii) Duties Owed to the Client Independent of Contract

The Defective Premises Act 1972

Replace paragraph 9-037 (to incorporate new text) with:

The duty set out in s.1 applies only to work taken on after the commencement **9-037**
date of the Act, which was 1 January 1974. The Act applies only to "dwellings".
The term is not defined in the Act. The term has been interpreted, for the purposes
of other legislation, as meaning a person's home (or one of his homes).[57] It has been
held that, for the purposes of the Act, a dwelling house is a building used or capable
of being used as a dwelling house, not being a building which is used predominantly
for commercial or industrial purposes.[58] The Act applies only to the provision of a
new dwelling, whether by the construction of a new building, the conversion of an
existing non-residential building or the enlargement of an existing building. Prior
to the commencement of the Building Safety Act 2022 it did not apply to the
renovation or refurbishment of an existing dwelling unless the effect is to create a
building "wholly different" from the old building.[59] Section 1 of the Act applies to
the failure to carry out necessary remedial work as well as to the carrying out of
work badly.[60] The duty under s.1 on a person taking on work "in connection with
the provision of a dwelling" does not extend to approved inspectors who had
provided building control services to ensure compliance with building regulations.[61]

[57] *Uratemp Ventures v Collins* [2001] UKHL 43; [2002] 1 A.C. 301, for the purposes of the Housing
Act 1988.

[58] *Catlin Estates Ltd v Carter Jonas* [2005] EWHC 2315; [2006] P.N.L.R. 15.

[59] *Jenson v Faux* [2011] EWCA Civ 423; [2011] 1 W.L.R. 3038. In *Rendlesham Estates Plc v Barr Ltd*
[2014] EWHC 3968 (TCC); [2015] 1 W.L.R. 3663, Edwards-Stuart J examined a number of important
issues arising under the Defective Premises Act 1972 and in the particular context of a building in
multiple ownership. He held that a "dwelling" is the place where a person or household lives to the exclusion of members of another household. Thus each apartment in a block of flats, together with its balcony,
comprised a dwelling but the common parts were not included. However, the construction of the
structural and common parts would amount to "work ... in connection with the provision of a dwelling" within the meaning of s.1 of the Act if those parts were physically or functionally connected with
the relevant dwelling (the apartment), especially when the apartment-owner had an obligation under its
lease to share the cost of maintenance and repair of the structural and common parts.

[60] In *Andrews v Schooling* [1991] 1 W.L.R. 783 CA the purchasers of a leasehold flat claimed damages against the freehold owners and developers from whom the flat was purchased on the basis that
the cellar was unfit for habitation through damp. The defendants had carried out no work to the cellar,
but were held liable under s.1 of the Act for failing to do so. The Defective Premises Act 1972 does not
impose a duty upon persons who build a dwelling for their own occupation, even if they later sell it on,
where the development is not part of a business venture: *Zennstrom v Fagot* [2013] EWHC 288 (TCC);
147 Con. L.R. 162.

[61] *Lessees and Management Co of Herons Court v Heronslea Ltd* [2018] EWHC 3309 (TCC); [2019]
B.L.R. 401. The decision was upheld on appeal—see [2019] EWCA Civ 1423; [2019] 1 W.L.R. 5849.

Replace paragraph 9-040 (to incorporate new text and footnote) with:

Subsection 1(5) provides that any cause of action under the section shall be **9-040**
deemed for limitation purposes to have accrued at the time when the dwelling was
completed. This has been interpreted as a "longstop" provision.[64] In *Payne v John
Setchell Ltd*,[65] Judge Lloyd QC held that a claim under the Defective Premises Act

does not amount to an "action for damages for negligence" within the meaning of s.14A of the Limitation Act 1980 (introduced by the Latent Damage Act 1986). Accordingly, a claimant under the Act does not have the benefit of an extension of time of three years from the date of knowledge subject to the long-stop of 15 years.[66] However, as a consequence of s.135 of the Building Safety Act 2022 the limitation period for claims under the Defective Premises Act 1972 is extended to 30 years for dwellings completed prior to 28 June 2022[66a] and 15 years for dwellings completed after that date.

[64] See the observations made in the Court of Appeal in *Alexander v Mercouris* [1979] 1 W.L.R. 1270 which were applied in *Catlin Estates Ltd v Carter Jonas* [2005] EWHC 2315 (TCC); [2006] P.N.L.R. 15.

[65] [2002] P.N.L.R. 7, approving the view adopted in the 4th edition of this work. For the facts, see para.9-087.

[66] This result would in any event follow from the construction of s.1(1) adopted in *Thompson v Clive Alexander & Partners* (1992) 28 Con. L.R. 49: a duty to ensure that a dwelling is fit for habitation goes beyond a duty to exercise reasonable skill and care. Subsection 1(5) contains an important proviso: if, after completion of the dwelling, further work is done to rectify defects in the original work, any cause of action in relation to such further work accrues only when it is finished. Thus in *Alderson v Beetham Organisation Ltd* [2003] EWCA Civ 408; [2003] 1 W.L.R. 1786 it was held that the leaseholders of flats acquired a fresh cause of action upon completion of the developer's ineffective works to remedy the originally installed but defective damp proof system in the building.

[66a] Albeit subject to the possibility of a defence pursuant to the European Convention on Human Rights—see s.135(5).

(b) Duties to Third Parties

(ii) Negligence

The type of loss

Replace footnote 119 with:

9-063 [119] The precise characterisation of the economic loss may be important for limitation purposes. In *Abbott v Will Gannon & Smith Ltd* [2005] EWCA Civ 198; 103 Con. L.R. 92; [2005] P.N.L.R. 30, structural engineers who had designed allegedly ineffective remedial works argued that the claimant owner had suffered economic loss upon completion of the remedial works, since the owner had then been in possession of a defective building which was worth less than it would have been had the remedial works been effective. The Court of Appeal rejected the argument, deciding that it was bound by the pre-*Murphy* decision of the House of Lords in *Pirelli General Cable Works Ltd v Oscar Faber & Partners* [1983] 2 A.C. 1 to hold that damage occurred only when cracks subsequently appeared in the building and that such damage was physical damage. The court also stated that if, contrary to its holding, the loss was properly characterised as economic loss, it was not suffered until the defect was discovered because only then would there be any depreciation in market value or cost of repairs. However, small differences in the underlying facts can produce a different outcome. In *BDW Trading Ltd v URS Corp Ltd* [2021] EWHC 2796 (TCC); 200 Con. L.R. 192 the issue was the date on which damage occurred for the purposes of claims that might have been brought against BDW by third parties. The Court accepted that the date of knowledge was not the date of accrual of the cause of action in tort (at [89]) but also accepted that *Pirelli* did not set out a complete code as to when damage occurs. In each case the issue is when is detriment suffered. The Court approved the reasoning on this issue in *Co-operative Group Ltd v Birse Developments Ltd (in liquidation)* [2014] EWHC 530 (TCC); [2014] B.L.R. 359 and held that this was not inconsistent with *Law Society v Sephton & Co* [2006] UKHL 22; [2006] 2 A.C. 543. Notwithstanding the decision in *Abbott*, the Court held in a latent defects case that the cause of action accrued no later than the date of practical completion (at [108]) and not when physical signs of damage (such as cracking) occurred. In a negligent design case (such as *BDW* which was a claim against structural engineers), if the structure is negligently designed such that remedial works will inevitably be required, the authors respectfully endorse the analysis of Fraser J in *BDW*.

The complex structure theory

Replace footnote 155 with:

155 Since *Murphy* a number of first instance courts rejected such arguments and the Court of Appeal **9-080** again considered a submission based upon the complex structure theory in *Bellefield Computer Services Ltd v E Turner & Sons Ltd* [2000] B.L.R. 97 CA. The claimant argued that it was entitled to recover for damage caused to parts of the dairy other than the storage area which was bounded by the inadequately constructed fire-stop wall because those parts of the building were put to different uses from the storage area. The argument was rejected and the decision of Bell J at first instance was upheld, albeit without comment upon the status of the complex structure theory as such. Schiemann LJ pointed out that it was unrealistic to regard parts of the diary as separate properties just because different parts were put to different uses: the dairy was constructed as one unit, marketed as a unit, bought for use as a unit and used by the claimant as a unit. Following Bellefield similar contentions were rejected in a number of first instance cases. The issue most clearly arose in *Broster v Galliard Docklands Ltd* [2011] EWHC 1722 (TCC); [2011] B.L.R. 569; [2011] P.N.L.R. 34. There, the purchasers from a developer of three newly constructed terraced townhouses brought a claim in tort against the contractor responsible for their design and construction. The houses shared a roof, which it was alleged had been defectively built with the result that it lifted in high winds and damaged the accommodation below. The purchasers argued that the roof was property separate from the houses beneath, invoking the complex structure theory. Akenhead J rejected the argument. He held that it was wholly artificial to regard the segment of the roof over each house as separate from the rest of the roof, or to regard the composite roof as separate from the construction beneath; conceptually, there was no significant difference between a common roof over a number of terraced units and a common foundation. Accordingly, the builder of the terrace owed no duty of care in tort to the purchasers of the individual units to safeguard against damage to any part of the terrace. The judge expressed doubt obiter as to whether the complex structure theory has a part to play in the law of negligence relating to buildings and structures; at any rate, it seems clear that the court will resist artificial structural subdivisions which are contrived so as to invoke the theory. An attempt to rely on *Murphy* failed on the facts in *Avantage (Cheshire) Ltd v GB Building Solutions Ltd* [2022] EWHC 171 (TCC); [2022] P.N.L.R. 13 at [115] where the Court expressed the provisional view (on a summary judgment application) that it was difficult to see how a consultant who provided a fire report could be said to have caused physical damage following a fire.

Reliance upon a statement

Replace paragraph 9-085 (to incorporate new text and footnotes) with:

No *Hedley Byrne* duty will be imposed in respect of reports or advice provided **9-085** for persons other than the claimant unless the defendant was, at least, aware that his report or advice might be so used.168 Similarly an express disclaimer will generally be effective to prevent a duty of care arising.169 However, the imposition of a duty is necessarily fact sensitive. In *Avantage (Cheshire) Ltd v GB Building Solutions Ltd,*169a the Court refused to strike out a claim in tort brought by an employer against a sub-contractor who had provided a fire engineering sign as it was arguable that the sub-contractor owed a duty of care to the employer notwithstanding the contractual framework and an express disclaimer in the retainer of the sub-consultant.169b

168 See *Rolls-Royce Power Engineering v Ricardo Consulting Engineers* [2003] EWHC 2871 (TCC); [2004] 2 All E.R. (Comm) 129; 98 Con. L.R. 169 (defendant engineers engaged to provide design services to a wholly-owned subsidiary of the claimant; the claimant acquired the subsidiary's business to the claimant and suffered loss due to defendants' allegedly negligent design; held that the defendant owed no duty of care in tort to avoid causing economic loss to the claimant, since the defendant was unaware of the claimant's interest and the claimant had not relied upon the defendant's design); *Offer-Hoar v Larkstore Ltd* [2006] EWHC 2742; [2006] P.N.L.R. 17 (geo-technical engineer which provided a site investigation report owed no duty of care to avoid causing economic loss to a subsequent developer of the site whose use of the report was not reasonably foreseeable. This finding was not challenged on the subsequent appeal [2006] EWCA Civ 1079; [2006] 1 W.L.R. 2926.

169 See, for examples: *Wolverine Tube (Canada) Inc v Noranda Metal Industries Ltd* (1995) 26 O.R. 577, ONCA (defendant prepared environmental reports for an industrial client under a contract which

provided that the reports were not be used outside the client's organisation without the defendant's permission; the reports each contained a clear disclaimer of liability to third parties; a purchaser from the defendant's client relied upon the reports; held that the disclaimers and the terms of the contract with the client were such as to prevent a duty of care from arising); *McKinlay Hendry Ltd v Tonkin Taylor Ltd* [2005] N.Z.L.R. 318, NZCA (an express disclaimer in the defendants' report, as well as the contractual arrangements put in place by the parties, precluded a finding that the defendants were liable for negligent misstatement in a ground investigation report which was relied upon by a party which was not their client). See also *BDW Trading Ltd v Integral Geotechnique (Wales) Ltd* [2018] EWHC 1915 (TCC); 179 Con. L.R. 112 (a contractual requirement for a consulting engineers' report to have been assigned to subsequent purchaser precluded a duty of care between the engineers and purchaser arising, even when no such assignment had, in fact, happened).

169a [2022] EWHC 171 (TCC); [2022] P.N.L.R. 13.

169b In *Rushbond Plc v the JS Design Partnership* [2021] EWCA Civ 1889; [2022] P.N.L.R. 9, the Court noted that there is a low threshold to overcome when seeking to establish that an alleged duty of care is arguable (at [42]). This is particularly the case where the alleged duty arises in circumstances where the courts have provided limited guidance.

3. THE STANDARD OF CARE

(b) General Practice and Knowledge as Evidence of the Standard

Exceptions to the general rule

In paragraph 9-111, replace list item "1." (to incorporate update to footnote 230) with:

9-111   1.   Cases in which the court considers that there is no logical basis for the body of opinion in accordance with which the defendant acted.230

230 In *Bolitho v City & Hackney HA* [1998] A.C. 232 HL a medical negligence case, Lord Browne-Wilkinson said:

> "the Court is not bound to hold that a defendant doctor escapes liability for negligent treatment or diagnosis just because he leads evidence from a number of medical experts who are genuinely of the opinion that the defendant's treatment or diagnosis accorded with sound medical practice. In the *Bolam* case itself, McNair J [1957] 1 W.L.R. 583, 587 stated that the defendant had to have acted in accordance with the practice accepted as proper by a '*responsible* body of medical men'. Later, at 588, he referred to 'a standard of practice recognised a proper by a competent *reasonable* body of opinion'. Again, in the passage which I have cited from *Maynard's case*, Lord Scarman refers to a 'respectable' body of professional opinion. The use of these adjectives—responsible, reasonable and respectable—all show that the court has to be satisfied that the exponents of the body of opinion relied upon can demonstrate that such opinion has a logical basis."

He concluded: "if, in a rare case, it can be demonstrated that the professional opinion is not capable of withstanding logical analysis, the judge is entitled to hold that the body of opinion is not reasonable or responsible." See also *Martlet Homes Ltd v Mulalley & Co Ltd* [2022] EWHC 1813 (TCC) which cited Edwards-Stuart J in *199 Knightsbridge Development Ltd v WSP UK Ltd* [2014] EWHC 43 (TCC) with approval stating that the argument (in the context of the installation of defective cladding) that "everyone else was doing it" does not, on a proper application of the "*Bolam*" principle, operate as a get out of jail free card.

(c) Expert Evidence

Replace footnote 238 with:

9-115   238 See *Pantelli Associates Ltd v Corporate City Developments Number Two Ltd* [2010] EWHC 3189 (TCC); [2011] P.N.L.R. 12 at [16]–[18] per Coulson J. The authors doubt whether this is a correct statement of the law. The better view of *Pantelli* may be that it is authority for the propositions that it may be an abuse of process either to commence proceedings without any belief in the truth of the contents of a pleaded case or with no intention of obtaining the expert evidence required to make that case good. This view is consistent with the decision of Akenhead J in *ACD (Landscape Architects) Ltd v Overall*

[2012] EWHC 100 (TCC); 140 Con. L.R. 82 (at [17]). In practice, expert evidence is often obtained by both parties when complying with the Pre-Action Protocol for Construction and Engineering Disputes. Particulars of Claim will not be struck out if no expert evidence is served (but has been obtained)—see *Crest Nicholson Operations Ltd v Grafik Architects Ltd* [2021] EWHC 2948 (TCC); 199 Con. L.R. 74.

5. DAMAGES

(a) Causation, duty nexus and legal responsibility for loss

(i) Causation

Concurrent causes

Replace footnote 467 with:

467 In *Greenwich Millennium Village Ltd v Essex Services Group Plc* [2013] EWHC 3059 (TCC); 151 Con. L.R. 1, Coulson J adopted that approach in holding that each of two separate workmanship defects was sufficient to cause the flooding in an apartment block. See also *Martlet Homes Ltd v Mulalley & Co Ltd* [2022] EWHC 1813 (TCC) where the judge applied the "effective cause" test and not the "but for" test.

9-214

(ii) Duty Nexus and the Scope of the Duty

Replace footnote 472 with:

472 [2021] UKSC 20; [2021] 3 W.L.R. 81 at [22]. This was applied in the context of a claim against a structural engineer in *BDW Trading Ltd v URS Corp Ltd* [2021] EWHC 2796 (TCC); 200 Con. L.R. 192 where it was said to be of general application to claims in negligence and not limited to advice cases (at [39]). The analysis in *BDW* is concerned with the question of whether, on assumed facts, a duty of care existed, but the editors respectfully suggest that the judge's approach neatly demonstrates that the close consideration of the "duty nexus" is as important to the determination of that question as it is to the ascertainment of the scope of duty. Depending on the facts, the questions may be addressing the same problem, namely: "what is the defendant's responsibility for a particular type of harm?"

9-216

Replace footnote 474 with:

474 In *Hancock v Tucker* [1999] Lloyd's Rep. P.N. 814 the defendant architect was engaged to design and seek planning permission for a scheme to convert his hotel into sheltered accommodation for the elderly. He alleged that, as a result of the defendant's negligence, he would have obtained planning permission for a suitable scheme two years earlier than in fact he did. By that time, the value of the property had fallen. The claimant sought to recover the difference between the values of the hotel with planning permission at the date when planning permission was granted and the date when it should have been granted. The defendant argued that this loss was caused by a fall in the property market and was outside the scope of his duty. Toulson J held that there had been no breach of duty by the defendant, but said that if there had, he would have found that loss caused by a fall in the market was within the scope of his duty. The defendant had advised the claimant as to which course he should take in the matter of seeking planning permission for the development of the property, knowing that the purpose for which he was retained was to enable the claimant to realise the maximum value of the property by selling it with the best planning permission which he could obtain in the shortest time. It was reasonably foreseeable that if the defendant was negligent, the claimant might lose a marketing opportunity which it was his purpose to obtain. Accordingly, the claimant would have recovered the loss claimed. For another example of the failure of an argument that the loss claimed was outside the scope of the defendant's duty, see *Try Build Ltd v Invicta Leisure (Tennis) Ltd* (2000) 71 Con. L.R. 140 (engineers' duty to certify the adequacy of sub-contractor's roof design and materials was not limited to protecting the main contractor against overpayment to the subcontractor; the duty arose before the engineers' contract was novated from the employer to the main contractor; had the engineers discharged their duty while still engaged by the employer, the subcontractor's design would not have been adopted and the loss claimed would have been avoided); In *John Grimes Partnership Ltd v Gubbins* [2013] EWCA Civ 37; [2013] B.L.R. 126; [2013] P.N.L.R. 17 the Court of Appeal readily held that a consulting engineer who delayed in completing design work was liable for losses attributable to downward movement in property values. The engineer knew (and anyway could reasonably foresee) that delay on his part would

9-218

delay completion of the development and so cause the developer loss if the property market fell in the interim. There was nothing in his contract of engagement, nor was there any general understanding or expectation in the property world, which indicated that the engineer had not assumed responsibility for such losses. The case is discussed at [2013] P.N. 128. In *BDW Trading Ltd v URS Corp Ltd* [2021] EWHC 2796 (TCC); 200 Con. L.R. 192, the Court held that reputational damages fall outside of the scope of duty of a structural engineer, alternatively were too remote (at [47], [62] and [64]).

(iii)   Legal Responsibility

Foreseeability

Replace paragraph 9-221 (to incorporate updates to footnotes 486 and 487) with:

9-221 In order to succeed, the claimant must establish not only that the damage was caused by the breach of duty of the architect, engineer or quantity surveyor, but also that it was foreseeable. If the claim is brought in contract, this means that the loss must either (a) arise naturally in the usual course of things from such a breach, or (b) have been in the contemplation of the parties at the time the contract was made as the probable result of the breach.[486] If the claim is brought in tort, it means that, at the time the breach of duty was committed, the damage (or at least the type of damage) was reasonably foreseeable as a consequence of the breach.[487] It may be that, in the light of the Court of Appeal's decision in *Wellesely Partners v Withers LLP*[488] this distinction will cease to matter in cases against construction procession- als because the contractual test will be adopted in any case where there is an engagement. If it is foreseeable that breach of duty will cause the type of loss which is in fact suffered, it is irrelevant that neither the extent nor the precise nature of the loss could have been foreseen.[489] Whether the foreseeable loss was of the same type as the loss suffered will be a question of fact in each case.[490] In rare cases argu- ments over the type of loss may be closely connected with when the loss occurred (for example, the nature of the loss changing as a result of changing external conditions).[491]

---

[486] *Hadley v Baxendale* (1854) 9 Exch. 341. In *Czarnikow Ltd v Koufos* [1969] 1 A.C. 350 at 388; and in *Balfour Beatty Construction (Scotland) Ltd v Scottish Power Plc* (1994) 71 B.L.R. 20 at 26, the House of Lords has said that the test in relation to the second limb was whether the loss was likely to occur "with a very substantial degree of probability". For a full discussion of the requirement of foresee- ability in contract, see J. Edelman and others (eds), *McGregor on Damages*, 21st edn (London: Sweet & Maxwell, 2021, 1st supp, 2021), Ch.8. In *Orchard Plaza Management Co Ltd v Balfour Beatty Regional Construction Ltd* [2022] EWHC 1490 (TCC); [2022] P.N.L.R. 24, the Court held in the context of a construction dispute that loss suffered by an assignee was in the reasonable contemplation of the parties at the time a contractual warranty was entered into (at [77]).

[487] For a full discussion of the requirement of foreseeability in tort, see *McGregor on Damages* (2021, 1st supp, 2021), Ch.8.

[488] [2016] P.N.L.R. 19.

[489] *H Parsons (Livestock) Ltd v Uttley Ingham & Co Ltd* [1978] 3 Q.B. 791 CA; *Brown v KMR Services Ltd* [1995] 2 Lloyd's Rep. 513 CA. cf. *Transfield Shipping Inc v Mercator Shipping Inc* [2008] UKHL 48, a shipping case, where the majority appeared willing to take into account that the unusual extent of the loss was not generally foreseeable by the defendant or the market and so was not recoverable.

[490] Thus, in *Balfour Beatty Construction (Scotland) Ltd v Scottish Power Plc* (1994) 71 B.L.R. 20 HL it was held that the demolition and reconstruction of an aqueduct was not a foreseeable consequence of the interruption of the electricity supply to the claimant's concrete batching plant. The electricity sup- plier did not know that the claimant had contracted to build the aqueduct using continuous pouring of concrete and so could not reasonably have foreseen the result of failure of the power supply. Demoli- tion of the aqueduct was a different type of loss from wastage of concrete or site resources, which were foreseeable results of loss of power.

[491] Such arguments were deployed in the New Zealand case of *Bevan Investments Ltd v Blackhall and*

Struthers (No.2) [1973] 2 N.Z.L.R. 45 (first instance); [1978] 2 N.Z.L.R. 97 (on appeal) and the Privy Council case of *Alcoa Minerals of Jamaica Inc v Herbert Broderick* [2002] 1 A.C. 371. In both cases it was argued that changing economic circumstances between the date of the breach and the date of the trial meant that the loss, as viewed at the trial date, was of a different type than the loss caused by the breach as viewed at that date. The argument was rejected in both cases.

(c)   Heads of Damage

(viii)   Personal Injuries

Replace footnote 556 with:

556 See W. Norris and others (eds), *Kemp & Kemp: The Quantum of Damages in Personal Injury and   **9-243** Fatal Accident Claims*, Rel.164 (London: Sweet & Maxwell, 2022).

CHAPTER 10

SURVEYORS

[63]

2.   GENERAL

(b)   Duties to Third Parties

(iii)   Other Liabilities

Deceit

Replace footnote 145 with:

10-050   [145] See the RICS Policy Wording which provides cover to "innocent" co-insureds of fraudsters, subject to certain terms; see further M. Cannon and B. McGurk, *Professional Indemnity Insurance*, 2nd edn (Oxford: Oxford University Press, 2016), para.8.39.

Defective Premises Act 1972

Replace footnote 150 with:

10-051   [150] Defective Premises Act 1972 s.1(1). See further para.9-033. And see also Defective Premises Act 1972 s.2A for the duty in relation to the taking on of work in relation to a building containing a dwelling.

4.   DAMAGES

(b)   Remoteness

Replace footnote 503 with:

10-148   [503] See J. Edelman and others (eds), *McGregor on Damages*, 21st edn (London: Sweet & Maxwell, 2021), Ch.8, para.8-061.

(c)   Scope of the Duty

Replace footnote 522 with:

10-154   [522] See *Manchester Building Society v Grant Thornton UK LLP* [2021] UKSC 20; [2021] W.L.R. 81 and para.10-159; and even in the context of valuers, this counterfactual is not universally appropriate:

see *Charles B Lawrence & Associates v Intercommercial Bank Ltd* [2021] UKPC 30; [2022] P.N.L.R. 7 at [19]—it is a "helpful cross-check" of the scope of the duty "in most but not all cases".

Replace footnote 538 with:

538 [2021] UKSC 20; [2021] 3 W.L.R. 81 at [27] per Lord Hodge and Lord Sales; see also *Charles B Lawrence & Associates v Intercommercial Bank Ltd* [2021] UKPC 30; [2022] P.N.L.R. 7 at [19].   **10-161**

Replace footnote 543 with:

543 Note that this, on its own, is now unlikely to be enough to make the adviser responsible for the entire   **10-164**
loss: see *Hughes-Holland v BPE Solicitors* [2017] UKSC 21; [2018] A.C. 599 at [50]–[52]; and *Manchester Building Society v Grant Thornton UK LLP* [2021] UKSC 20; [2021] W.L.R. 81 at [20]–[22] and [94]. In *Charles B Lawrence & Associates v Intercommercial Bank Ltd* [2021] UKPC 30; [2022] P.N.L.R. 7, the Privy Council treated a recovery made from conveyancing attorneys as attributable to their failure to identify defective title and therefore not commensurate with the loss attributable to the surveyor's overvaluation.

After paragraph 10-170, add new paragraph:

In *Charles B Lawrence & Associates v Intercommercial Bank Ltd*, the Privy   **10-170A**
Council held that the valuer was responsible only for that part of the loss that reflected the overvaluation that arose following the erroneous assumption of commercial rather than residential use, and did not extend to the full loss incurred because of a defect in title that rendered the security worthless.554a

554a [2021] UKPC 30; [2022] P.N.L.R. 7.

(d)   Measure of Damages

(iii)   *Negligent Survey or Valuation for Lender*

Assessment of the scope of the duty

Replace footnote 715 with:

715 Or applying the approach in *Manchester Building Society v Grant Thornton UK LLP* [2021] UKSC   **10-210**
20; [2021] W.L.R. 81, the loss that represents the fruition of the risk that it was the purpose of the valuer's duty to protect the lender against: see [17]; and see also *Charles B Lawrence & Associates v Intercommercial Bank Ltd* [2021] UKPC 30; [2022] P.N.L.R. 7 at [14]–[15].

(vii)   *Physical Injury, Inconvenience and Distress*

Quantum of damages

Replace footnote 791 with:

791 The Court of Appeal will apply the principles reiterated by the House of Lords in *Pickett v British*   **10-235**
Rail Engineering Ltd [1980] A.C. 136. See also the commentary in W. Norris and others (eds), *Kemp & Kemp, The Quantum of Damages in Personal Injury and Fatal Accident Claims*, Rel.164 (London: Sweet & Maxwell, 2022), Vol.1 Ch.19.

(viii)   *Incidental Expenses*

Replace footnote 829 with:

829 See *McGregor on Damages* (2021), Ch.34, para.34-062: "It is, however, difficult to see the basis for   **10-239**
this … denial of recovery. For on the assumption that the claimant would not have bought the property had the defendant submitted a true report, the cost of neither purchase nor resale would have been incurred by him. True, he had contemplated incurring costs in purchasing a house, but such costs will still have to be incurred by him in acquiring a substitute for the defective house now disposed of."

5.   SHARED RESPONSIBILITY

(a)   Contributory Negligence

The impact of SAAMCO

Replace footnote 854 with:

10-249   [854] Note that Lord Millett envisaged that a deduction *might* be appropriate to the over-valuation, as well as to the overall loss, where the lender's negligence has caused or contributed directly to the overvaluation: [2000] 2 A.C 190 at 215B–215C. *Charles B Lawrence & Associates v Intercommercial Bank Ltd* [2021] UKPC 30; [2022] P.N.L.R. 7 appears to be a case in which the deduction of contributory negligence was made to that part of the loss for which the valuer was liable, rather than to the overall loss. However, the point was not discussed in the Privy Council.

CHAPTER 11

SOLICITORS

1. GENERAL

Regulation

Replace paragraph 11-003 (to incorporate updates to footnotes 10 and 16) with:

11-003   Solicitors are regulated by the Solicitors Regulation Authority.[9] The applicable rules are contained in the SRA Standards and Regulations 2019.[10] More serious cases of alleged misconduct are determined by the Solicitors Disciplinary Tribunal, which is a statutory tribunal independent of the Solicitors Regulation Authority.[11] The courts have power, known as the "Hamid jurisdiction" (after *R. (on the application of Hamid) v Secretary of State for the Home Department*)[12] to refer a solicitor to the SRA for misconduct in the form of abusing the court's processes. Under the Legal Services Act 2007 a Legal Services Board was established to supervise the work of the approved regulators.[13] Solicitors who carry on investment business are subject to the Financial Services and Markets Act 2000.[14] All solicitors have to be insured with qualifying insurers and the insurance must comply with certain minimum terms and conditions.[15] For a general discussion of the solicitors' profession and its regulation, reference should be made to *Cordery on Legal Services*[16] and the SRA Standards and Regulations.[17]

[9] In 2007, the Law Society delegated to the Solicitors Regulation Authority powers it was granted under the Solicitors Act 1974 and Legal Services Act 2007. Such powers permit the Authority to develop and enforce rules regarding the education, admission, registration, and practise requirements of solicitors. See para.11-001 as to the legal role of solicitors. See too, the Solicitors Act 1974 ss.31 and 79–80; Administration of Justice Act 1985 ss.9 and 9A, and the Legal Services Act 2007 s.83 and Sch.4, as applicable.

[10] These came into force on 25 November 2019. The most important of these are the Principles, with seven fundamental tenets of ethical behaviour, the Code of Conduct for Solicitors, RELs and RFLs, the Code of Conduct for Firms, and the Accounts Rules. Before 2007 regulation was by the Law Society, and the applicable rules could be found in the *Guide to the Professional Conduct of Solicitors*. The last printed edition was the eighth in 1999. This was replaced by the Solicitors' Code of Conduct 2007 and then the Solicitors' Code of Conduct 2011. From 2011 to 2019, the Solicitors Regulation Authority published successive versions of *The SRA Handbook*, of which the profession's 2011 Code of Conduct formed a part: for a brief history of the regulatory framework, and recent reforms see I. Miller and others (eds), *Cordery on Legal Services*, 9th edn, Issue 129 (London: LexisNexis, 2022), Div. A and Div. E, 1D and A. Hooper and G. Treverton-Jones, *Outcomes-Focused Regulation* (London: Law Society Publishing, 2011). Significantly, the rules have the force of law, see, in relation to the previous Solicitors Practice Rules 1990, *Westlaw Services Ltd v Boddy* [2010] EWCA Civ 929; [2011] P.N.L.R. 4 and cases referred to therein. Complaints about poor service are dealt with by the Legal Services Ombudsman. The SRA has powers to intervene in a solicitor's practice, which was formerly the responsibility of the Law Society. The Court of Appeal in *Holder v Law Society* [2003] EWCA Civ 39; [2003] 3 All E.R. 62 held that this power raised no issue under the Human Rights Act 1998.

[11] See *https://www.sra.org.uk/solicitors/*; *https://www.solicitorstribunal.org.uk/about-us*; and *https://www.solicitorstribunal.org.uk/constitutions-and-procedures* [all accessed 1 October 2021].

[12] [2012] EWHC 3070 (Admin); [2013] C.P. Rep. 6. The *Hamid* case related to persistent filing by a firm of solicitors of unmeritorious and late applications in relation to immigration overstayers, and culminated in the court warning that future breaches would culminate in the courts referring lawyers to the SRA. Such a reference was made in *Re Sandbrook Solicitors* [2015] EWHC 2473 (Admin); [2016] P.N.L.R. 2 (where unmeritorious applications for judicial review had been pursued. The jurisdiction is explained in detail in *R. (on the applications of Sathivel v Secretary of State for the Home Department)* [2018] EWHC 913 (Admin); [2018] 4 W.L.R. 89, another case concerning late applications in immigration cases (where references to the SRA were made). More recently, the jurisdiction was used in a case involving solicitors failing to put all relevant material before the court (despite the applicants owing a duty of candour), misusing an urgent procedure and acting without instructions: *DVP v Secretary of State for the Home Department* [2021] EWHC 606 (Admin); [2021] 4 W.L.R. 75. In the *DVP* case, the court accepted apologies from the legal representatives involved in the case and declined to make a referral. Although the *Hamid* jurisdiction originated in the Administrative Court, it was applied in a libel case in the Queen's Bench Division in *Gubarev v Orbis Business Intelligence Ltd* [2020] EWHC 2167 (QB); [2020] 4 W.L.R 122, where solicitors had passed on a zoom link to a hearing in contravention of a court order. In the latter case, the court held that it would have referred the solicitors to the SRA but for the fact they had already self-referred.

[13] See *https://legalservicesboard.org.uk/about-us/approved-regulators* [Accessed 1 October 2021].

[14] See further the Solicitors' Financial Services (Scope) Rules 2018, and the Solicitors' Financial Services (Conduct of Business) Rules 2018. The Law Society is a designated professional body under the Act, and firms may carry out certain regulated activities without being regulated by the Financial Services Authority. See further paras 14-021 and 14-022.

[15] See Ch.8 and M. Cannon and B. McGurk, *Professional Indemnity Insurance*, 2nd edn (Oxford: Oxford University Press, 2016), Ch.1 for an introduction.

[16] I. Miller and others (eds), *Cordery on Legal Services*, 9th edn, Issue 129 (London: LexisNexis, 2022).

[17] *https://www.sra.org.uk/solicitors/standards-regulations* [Accessed 1 October 2021]. See too, J. Gould and others, *The Law of Legal Services and Practice*, 2nd edn (London: LexisNexis, 2019), Chs 1 and 3 for commentary on this.

(a) Duties to Client

(i) Contractual Duties

Implied retainer

Replace footnote 28 with:

11-005 [28] [2016] EWHC 150 (Ch). See also *NDH Properties Ltd v Lupton Fawcett LLP* [2020] EWHC 3056 (Ch); [2021] P.N.L.R. 8 (where there was no conduct consistent only with there being a retainer, quite the contrary, and the fact that the solicitors acted for a client with opposed interests was a strong indication against a retainer); and *McDonnell v DASS Legal Solutions (MK) Law Ltd* [2022] EWHC 991 (QB); [2022] Costs L.R. 855 (choosing not to enter into a retainer when the parties could have done so indicates that an implied retainer was unlikely, and an implied retainer should not be imposed for convenience. There, the solicitor regarded the claimant as a client, but on an objective construction of the facts he was not).

Replace heading footnote 39 with:

The nature of the duties[39]

11-007 [39] The Code of Conduct 2007 r.2.02 set out matters which needed to be identified, including the client's objectives, and the solicitor's and the client's responsibilities. The Code of Conduct 2011 was less prescriptive, but see IB1.4. The two 2019 SRA Codes of Conduct further simplify the principles, but see para.8.6. W. Flenley, T. Leech and others in *The Law of Solicitors' Negligence and Liability*, 4th edn (London: Bloomsbury Professional, 2020) argue, at Ch.2, para.2.15, that the House of Lords decided in *Hilton v Barker Booth & Eastwood* [2005] 1 W.L.R. 567 that r.6 of the Solicitors Practice Rules 1990 (no longer in force) was a contractual term of the retainer, but that the case should not be treated as authority that there would be a contractual term that a solicitor should comply with the Practice Rules or Code of Conduct.

Replace paragraph 11-007 (to incorporate updates to footnotes 39 and 41) with:

In practice, the solicitor's failure to carry out some necessary step is normally treated as a breach of the general duty to exercise skill and care rather than a breach of some specific duty implied in the retainer.[40] In most cases it is submitted that this is the correct approach, although the duty of skill and care implies a number of general obligations.[41] In *Minkin v Landsberg*,[42] (a case about whether a limited retainer had been agreed in the context of a matrimonial finance dispute) Jackson LJ summarised the principles as follows:

"i) A solicitor's contractual duty is to carry out the tasks which the client has instructed and the solicitor has agreed to undertake.

ii) It is implicit in the solicitor's retainer that he/she will proffer advice which is reasonably incidental to the work that he/she is carrying out.

iii) In determining what advice is reasonably incidental, it is necessary to have regard to all the circumstances of the case, including the character and experience of the client.

iv) In relation to iii), it is not possible to give definitive guidance, but one can give fairly bland illustrations. An experienced businessman will not wish to pay for being told that which he/she already knows. An impoverished client will not wish to pay for advice which he/she cannot afford. An inexperienced client will expect to be warned of risks which are (or should be) apparent to the solicitor but not to the client.

v) The solicitor and client may, by agreement, limit the duties which would otherwise form part of the solicitor's retainer. As a matter of good practice the solicitor should confirm such agreement in writing. If the solicitor does not do so, the court may not accept that any such restriction was agreed."

In *Minkin*, the solicitor was instructed to draft a consent order in matrimonial proceedings, and owed the client, an intelligent woman who had practised as an accountant, no duty to advise her on the merits of the settlement or warnings as to its consequences. While the limited nature of the retainer was not confirmed in writing, contrary to good practice, the judge accepted that the retainer was limited.

[40] See, e.g. *Sykes v Midland Bank Executor & Trustee Co Ltd* [1971] 1 Q.B. 113 at 125H: failure to advise on lease; *County Personnel (Employment Agency) Ltd v Alan R Pulver & Co* [1987] 1 W.L.R. 916: failure to advise on unusual term in lease. For a different view see *Midland Bank v Hett, Stubbs & Kemp* [1979] Ch. 384 at 435A–435B per Oliver J.

[41] See also para.11-088. Note that the client will not owe any implied contractual duty of good faith to the solicitor. see *Candey Ltd v Basem Bosheh* [2021] EWHC 3409 (Comm); [2022] 4 W.L.R. 12.

[42] [2015] EWCA Civ 1152; [2016] 1 W.L.R. 1489 at [38]. See also the following: *Groom v Crocker* [1939] 1 K.B. 194 at 222: "The retainer when given puts into operation the normal terms of the contractual relationship, including in particular the duty of the solicitor to protect the client's interest and carry out his instructions in the matters to which the retainer relates, by all proper means. It is an incident of that duty that the solicitor shall consult with his client on all questions of doubt which do not fall within the express or implied discretion left him, and shall keep the client informed to such an extent as may be reasonably necessary according to the same criteria." per Scott LJ; *Midland Bank v Hett, Stubbs & Kemp* [1979] Ch. 384 at 402H: "The extent of his duties depends upon the terms and limits of that retainer and any duty of care to be implied must be related to what he is instructed to do." Per Oliver J. The analysis in *Minkin* was affirmed by the Court of Appeal in *Spire Property Development LLP v Withers LLP* [2022] EWCA Civ 970; [2022] P.N.L.R. 27.

(iii) Fiduciary Duties

General

Replace footnote 79 with:

[79] This classification is to an extent one of convenience only. Categories (2) to (5) are all aspects of the **11-014** same general principle. Another example is acting when there is a conflict of interest because the client may have a claim against the solicitor. Thus in the Australian case of *Atanaskovic Hartnell v Birketu Pty Ltd* [2021] NSWCA 201; (2021) 105 N.S.W.L.R. 542 a firm of solicitors acted for a client who was defrauded by one of the firm's employees to investigate a claim against the company's bank. There was a clear conflict of interest as the firm may have been vicariously liable for the solicitor. The firm had not obtained the client's fully informed consent to their acting, and in any event the conflict was so profound that they could not act for it. As a result, they were denied recovery of their fees under the Court's inherent jurisdiction.

Replace footnote 139 with:

(7) Confidence[139]

[139] See also paras 2-256 to 2-260 and paras 17-047 and 17-048. See generally, C.M. Phipps, S.T. **11-025** Teasdale and W.R. Harman, *Toulson and Phipps on Confidentiality*, 4th edn (London: Sweet Maxwell, 2020) and C. Hollander and S. Salzedo, *Conflicts of Interest*, 6th edn (London: Sweet Maxwell, 2020).

(iv) Trust Duties

Trusts in favour of a third party

Replace paragraph 11-037 (to incorporate updates to footnotes 201 and 203) with:
Solicitors may incur liability to a third party for funds which are held if they give **11-037** a solicitors' undertaking to use the funds for a specific purpose. In *Twinsectra v Yardley*,[201] the House of Lords held that when solicitors receive monies from a lender on an undertaking that they will be retained until they are applied in the acquisition of property on behalf of the client, and will only be used for that

purpose, a trust was created. The power to apply the money "in the acquisition of property" was sufficiently certain to create a trust, and the fact that the lender had not intended to create a trust was irrelevant. In contrast, in *Challinor v Juliet Bellis & Co*,[202] where there was no undertaking, no trust arose. On a detailed analysis of the facts the Court of Appeal held that investors paid money to the defendant solicitors as immediate loans to their clients. Briggs LJ set out the relevant principles applicable to *Quistclose* trusts,[203] in particular that property is transferred on terms which do not leave it at the free disposal of the transferee, and an intention to create a trust should be objectively construed and turns on the true construction of the words used.

[201] [2002] UKHL 12; [2002] 2 A.C. 164.

[202] [2015] EWCA Civ 59; [2016] W.T.L.R. 43. Similarly, in *Green Light Solutions Corp v Baker* 2021 BCCA 287; [2021] 12 W.W.R 606 monies were paid by the lender client's borrower to the solicitor, who transferred them on to the client. The solicitor was not told that there were conditions of the payment, indeed his client said that there were none, and he was not a trustee and not in breach of trust.

[203] [2015] EWCA Civ 59; [2016] W.T.L.R. 43 at [56]–[65]. A Quistclose trust is a form of resulting trust that comes into existence when monies are transferred for a particular purpose and that purpose fails. For an introduction, see P. Matthews, C. Mitchell, J. Harris, and S. Agnew (eds), *Underhill and Hayton Law Relating to Trusts and Trustees*, 20th edn (London: LexisNexis, 2022), Ch.1, art.1.37 and Ch. 8, art.27; W. Swadling (ed.), *The Quistclose Trust: Critical Essays* (Oxford: Hart Publishing 2004); and R. Chambers, *Resulting Trusts* (Oxford: Clarendon Press, 1997).

(b)   Duties to Third Parties

(i)   General

Reliance without retainer to quasi-client

Replace footnote 223 with:

11-043   [223]   (1989) 5 P.N. 103. Similarly, for *Mathew v Maughold Life Assurance Co Ltd* [1955–1995] P.N.L.R. 51 CA. It is submitted that *Crossnan* is still good law on any of the modern tests. To similar effect see *Bartle v GE Custodians* [2010] 1 N.Z.L.R. 802 High Court, where a solicitor owed a duty before a retainer had been formed when he was relied on for advice. In *Spire Property Development LLP v Withers LLP* [2022] EWCA Civ 970; [2022] P.N.L.R. 27 solicitors had acted for the claimant in the purchase of two properties for development. Two years later it was discovered that there were high voltage cables under the sites. The client asked the solicitors questions about the cables, which it answered and thus assumed a duty of care to the client. On the construction of the emails, the solicitors assumed no wider duty as to the client's remedies with respect to the cables.

(ii)   Liability to Beneficiaries without Reliance

Replace footnote 262 with:

11-050   [262]   [1995] 2 A.C. 207. For commentaries on this important decision, see J. Brady "Solicitors' duty of care in the drafting of will" (1995) 46 N.I.L.Q. 434; J. Dwyer "A comedy of errors" [1996] Tort L.R. 77; Evans, *Lawyers' Liabilities* (2002), Ch.1; T. Weir, "A Damnosa Hereditas" (1995) 111 L.Q.R. 357. See also T. Rosen Peacocke: "The remedy in White v Jones cases: smoothing the analytical wrinkles" (2008) 24 P.N. 138 for an argument that the principles of the case have been misapplied subsequently. For a recent analysis, see J. Lee and J. Skillen, "White & Jones (1995): A Legacy of the Search for Principle" in B. Sloan, *Landmark Cases in Succession Law* (Oxford: Hart Publishing, 2019), Ch.7.

(iii)   Duty of Care to the Other Side

Judicial comments on Gran Gelato

Replace footnote 318 with:

11-062   [318]   [2018] EWCA Civ 1082; [2019] Ch. 273 at [70]. In *Ashraf v Lester Dominic Solicitors Ltd* [2022]

EWHC 621 (Ch); [2022] P.N.L.R. 18 the signature of the deceased (the claimant being his executrix) was allegedly forged on a TR1 transferring property to a third party. The seventh defendant solicitors acted for a bank which proposed to loan money to the third party, and obtained registration of its charge by forwarding the TR1 to the Land Registry. Relying on *Gran Gelato*, *NRAM* and *P&P Property Ltd*, the Court held that it owed no duty to the deceased. Similarly, the first defendant solicitors, whose only involvement was to witness the purported signature of the deceased, owed no duty to protect the deceased if the person signing turned out to be a fraudster.

(iv)   Solicitors' Liability on Undertakings

Examples of undertakings

Replace paragraph 11-072 (to incorporate updates to footnotes 353 and 359) with:

Undertakings were given in the capacity of a solicitor in the following circumstances[353]: to hold money or deeds to another's order in relation to a property transaction where the solicitor was engaged[354]; to repay money to a third party in the event that negotiations for an agreement between the third party and the solicitor's client did not result in agreement by a particular date[355]; to a client's former solicitors not to release client moneys until a dispute over unpaid fees had been sorted out[356]; and in litigation to the claimant's solicitor that their client's directors would provide security by creating second charges in the claimant's favour on their own properties.[357] Undertakings will not be given in the capacity of a solicitor in the following circumstances: to hold or pay money in relation to the lease of a solicitor's office, or an undertaking on leaving a firm not to work for any client of the firm for a period of time[358]; to repay an advance of money for a client by a certain date with interest[359]; to repay moneys due to the claimant from a third party and a guarantee of a third party's obligation to repay a loan to the claimant with interest (when there was no element of actual contemplated work or services in the capacity of a solicitor).[360]

11-072

[353] And see also *The Crimdon* [1900] P. 171 (to enter an appearance in a proposed action and to give bail not exceeding the value of their client's ship and cargo in order to avoid its arrest); *Re Kerly, Son and Verden* [1901] 1 Ch. 467 (to acknowledge service for a defendant); *Re a Solicitor Ex p. Hales* [1907] 2 K.B. 539, Div Court (to pay over funds given to the solicitor for a particular purpose); *Re Coolgardie Goldfields Ltd* [1900] 1 Ch. 475 Ch. D. (to pay stamp duties and penalties in relation to documents used in evidence which were not stamped); *Swyny v Harland* [1894] 1 Q.B. 707 CA (to repay costs if an appeal was successful); *Attorney General v Emerson* (1889) 24 QBD 56 CA (as the solicitor of successful defendants to repay costs if the plaintiff's appeal succeeds); *Re Pass* (1887) 35 W.R. 410, CA (to pay over moneys recovered in litigation); *Re A Solicitor* [1966] 1 W.L.R. 1604 (to a bank to hold leases to the order of the bank and to account for the proceeds when sold); and *Atanaskovic Hartnell v Birketu Pty Ltd* [2021] NSWCA 201; (2021) 105 N.S.W.L.R. 54 (a promise not to charge client for work; quaere whether that would be a solicitor's undertaking in this jurisdiction).

[354] *Harcus Sinclair LLP v Your Lawyers Ltd* [2021] UKSC 32; [2021] 3 W.L.R. 598; [2021] P.N.L.R. 26 at [104] and [114].

[355] *United Mining and Finance Corp v Becher* [1910] 2 K.B. 296 KBD, cited with approval by *Harcus Sinclair LLP v Your Lawyers Ltd* [2021] UKSC 32; [2021] 3 W.L.R. 598; [2021] P.N.L.R. 26 at [107], as were the next two examples.

[356] *John Fox v Bannister King & Rigbeys* [1988] Q.B. 925; [1987] 3 W.L.R. 480.

[357] *Udall v Capri Lighting Ltd* [1988] Q.B. 907; [1987] 3 W.L.R. 465.

[358] Both of these examples are given in *Harcus Sinclair LLP v Your Lawyers Ltd* [2021] UKSC 32; [2021] 3 W.L.R. 598; [2021] P.N.L.R. 26 at [104] and [107].

[359] *Geoffrey Silver & Drake v Baines* [1971] 1 Q.B. 396 cited in *Harcus Sinclair LLP v Your Lawyers Ltd* [2021] UKSC 32; [2021] 3 W.L.R. 598; [2021] P.N.L.R. 26 at [108], as was the next example,

360 See *Ruparel v Awan* [2001] Lloyd's Rep. P.N. 258 Ch D, followed (in the context of a coverage dispute) in *Halliwells LLP v NES Solicitors* [2011] EWHC 947 (QB); [2011] P.N.L.R. 30.

Practice and procedure: the court's supervisory jurisdiction

Replace paragraph 11-078 (to incorporate updates to footnotes 400 and 404) with:

11-078   The courts' power to enforce summarily undertakings given by solicitors is part of the general jurisdiction of the courts to control solicitors' obligations, which is not confined to any fixed classification.[399] The court's supervisory jurisdiction over its officers only applies to a person admitted as a solicitor, and thus whilst it applies to individuals and firms, it does not apply to LLPs or limited companies, nor to other providers of legal services.[400] The jurisdiction is not for the purpose of enforcing legal rights, but to ensure honourable conduct on the part of the court's officers.[401] A failure to implement an undertaking is prima facie to be regarded as misconduct.[402] The general nature of the jurisdiction to enforce solicitors' undertakings was summarised by Balcombe LJ in *Udall v Capri Lighting Ltd*,[403] and Lord Briggs in *Harcus Sinclair LLP v Your Lawyers Ltd*.[404] The summary jurisdiction to enforce solicitors' undertakings also exists in Canada,[405] Australia,[406] and New Zealand.[407] In *John Fox v Bannister King & Rigbeys*, Sir John Donaldson MR reaffirmed that the summary character of the jurisdiction lay not in the burden or standard of proof, but in the procedure.[408] Claims invoking the supervisory jurisdiction of the court are often made pursuant to CPR Pt 8. The Court has a discretion as to the procedure to be adopted and often there are no pleadings, disclosure or oral evidence.[409] However, in an appropriate case the court can resolve issues of fact with the assistance of oral evidence and cross-examination, and can order pleadings and discovery.[410] As a consequence of its summary nature, the court will only exercise its jurisdiction in a clear case, see *Silver and Drake v Baines*.[411] The application should be entitled in the matter of the solicitor, rather than with the title of the action.[412] If the undertaking was made to the Court of Appeal, the application should be to that court.[413] An undertaking to a county court can be enforced in that court by committal.[414] An application for committal will normally result in an order for enforcement rather than for committal.[415] If the undertaking does not provide a period within which the act is to be done, it may be necessary to apply to the court first for an order fixing such a period.[416] It is not necessary to prove service of the undertaking on the respondent before an application for committal.[417]

399 *Harcus Sinclair LLP v Your Lawyers Ltd* [2021] UKSC 32; [2021] 3 W.L.R. 598; [2021] P.N.L.R. 26 at [94]. The statutory basis for the disciplinary jurisdiction of solicitors in the High Court or above is the Solicitors Act 1974 s.50, and below that is County Courts Act 1984 s.142 (which gives the County Court the same powers as regards undertakings as the High Court).

400 See the obiter comments in *Assaubayev v Michael Wilson & Partners Ltd* [2014] EWCA Civ 1491; [2015] P.N.L.R. 8. While it considered that there were reasons why the jurisdiction should extend more widely, the Supreme Court declined to make any decision doing so in *Harcus Sinclair LLP v Your Lawyers Ltd* [2021] UKSC 32; [2021] 3 W.L.R. 598; [2021] P.N.L.R. 26 at [142] and [143]. In that case, the undertaking given by the solicitor was on behalf of the corporate entity (i.e. the LLP), see [146]–148].

401 *Harcus Sinclair LLP v Your Lawyers Ltd* [2021] UKSC 32; [2021] 3 W.L.R. 598; [2021] P.N.L.R. 26 at [100].

402 *Harcus Sinclair LLP v Your Lawyers Ltd* [2021] UKSC 32; [2021] 3 W.L.R. 598; [2021] P.N.L.R. 26 at [101].

403 [1988] Q.B. 907 at 916C–918D.

404 [2021] UKSC 32; [2022] A.C. 783; [2021] P.N.L.R. 26 at [94]–[104].

405 e.g. *115 Place Co-operative Housing Association v Burke, Tomchenko, Duprat* (1994) 116 D.L.R. (4th) 657.

[406] e.g. *Wade v Licardy* (1993) 33 N.S.W.L.R. 1, Bryson J.

[407] e.g. *Countrywide Banking Corp Ltd v Kingston* [1990] 1 N.Z.L.R. 629.

[408] [1988] 1 Q.B. 925 at 931H.

[409] *Harcus Sinclair LLP Your Lawyers Ltd* [2021] UKSC 32; [2021] 3 W.L.R. 598; [2021] P.N.L.R. 26 at [99].

[410] *John Fox v Bannister King & Rigbeys* [1988] Q.B. 925 at 930E–930F per Nicholls LJ and 931H per Donaldson MR.

[411] [1971] 1 Q.B. 396 at 403B–403C per Lord Denning MR and at 403A–403E per Megaw LJ.

[412] According to the headnote of *Re Kerly, Son and Verden* [1901] 1 Ch. 467.

[413] As in *Jonesco v Evening Standard Co Ltd* [1932] 2 K.B. 340.

[414] County Courts Act 1984 s.142.

[415] *Re a Solicitor* [1966] 1 W.L.R. 1604.

[416] See *Cotton v Heyl* [1930] 1 Ch. 510 (where the undertaking was not by a solicitor).

[417] *Re Launder* (1908) 98 L.T. 554 (where the undertaking was not by a solicitor).

(c) The Standard of Skill and Care

(ii) *General Practice as Evidence of Reasonable Skill and Care*

An illustration: taking instructions

Replace footnote 487 with:

[487] [1997] P.N.L.R. 392. For similar reliance on the Guide see *Omega Trust Co Ltd v Wright Son & Pepper (No.2)* [1998] P.N.L.R. 337 at 347D per Douglas Brown J, and *Mortgage Express v Bowerman* [1996] 2 All E.R. 836 at 842a–842d per Sir Thomas Bingham MR. Cf. *Lennon v Englefield* [2021] EWHC 1473 (QB); [2021] Lloyd's Rep F.C. 432; [2022] P.N.L.R. 3, where the solicitors failure to carry out identity checks on their client in breach of the code of conduct and the Money Laundering Regulations 2007 did not mean that there was any breach of duty to her, as the provision were for the benefit of the public and not the client, and to similar effect *P&P Property Ltd v Owen White & Catlin* and *LLP Dreamvar v Mishcon de Reya* [2018] EWCA Civ 1082; [2018] P.N.L.R. 29 at [30], [31] and [78]. **11-099**

(vi) *General Observations*

When illegality taints a claim

Replace footnote 533 with:

[533] [2020] UKSC 42; [2021] 1 All ER Comm 1139; [2021] P.N.L.R. 6. For helpful commentaries see J. O'Sullivan, "Illegality and tort in the Supreme Court" (2021) 80 C.L.J. 215, and M. Pooles: "Stoffel & Co v Grondona" (2021) 37 P.N. 165. **11-111**

(e) Solicitor's Liability for Costs

Procedure

Replace paragraph 11-133 (to incorporate updates to footnotes 638 and 641) with:

Thirdly, the Court of Appeal held in *Ridehalgh* any procedure should be fair, **11-133** simple, and summary, avoiding elaborate proceedings, or formal discovery, and with the length of the hearings measured in hours.[638] The court must be astute to control what could be a costly form of satellite litigation. The effect of the summary nature of the wasted costs jurisdiction and the costs of an application have been considered in a number of cases. The Court of Appeal have held that allegations involving full scale relitigation of the issues in the original trial and which involved dishonesty should not proceed,[639] that the jurisdiction was inappropriate where there needed to be a detailed investigation of the facts or dishonesty was alleged, as such matters were not capable of summary determination,[640] that a wasted costs application was inappropriate if it would result in complex proceedings involving detailed investigations of fact,[641] that the wasted costs jurisdiction should not be used to generate substantial additional costs in satellite litigation which was as expensive and complex as the original litigation,[642] and that it would rarely be appropriate to grant an adjournment to investigate whether the client was willing to waive privilege, as that would create complexity and delay.[643] In the context of the inherent jurisdiction which exists in New Zealand, the Privy Council in *Harley v McDonald*[644] opined that allegations should be confined strictly to questions which are apt for summary disposal by the Court. However, in *Wagstaff v Colls (Wasted Costs Order)*,[645] the Court of Appeal held that fact that complex issues might arise in the wasted costs application did not preclude use of the procedure, and account had to be taken of the prospects of success and how far time could be saved by appropriate case management.

[638] See now CPR Pt 48 PD at para.53.5., which echoes this, a point reiterated in *Hedrich v Standard Bank London Ltd* [2008] EWCA Civ 905; [2009] P.N.L.R. 3. Where the amount of money is small, an oral hearing may not be necessary, but fairness required it when there were disputed facts, see *Gill v Humanwave Europe Ltd* [2010] EWCA Civ 799; [2010] I.C.R. 1343. While in most circumstances cross-examination of the representative against whom costs are sought will be inappropriate, the Court had jurisdiction to permit it, and it may be proportionate and fair in some circumstances, see *Godfrey Morgan v Cobalt* [2011] 6 Costs L.R. 1006, where cross-examination was correctly permitted as the representative no longer acted for the party, privilege had been waived, an oral hearing had been fixed, and there was a conflict on the facts. In *Hunt v Annolight Ltd* [2021] EWCA Civ 1663; [2022] 1 W.L.R. 701 the Court of Appeal made clear that the power to require the legal representative to attend for cross-examination was exceptional rather than the rule and gave guidance as to the matters which required consideration before doing so. The summary nature of the procedure means that a court does not have to be satisfied document by document that the impugned litigation was made at the instigation of the person against whom the wasted costs order is sought, see *MA Lloyd & Son Ltd (In Administration) v PPC International Ltd (t/a Professional Powercraft)* [2016] EWHC 2162 (QB); [2017] P.N.L.R. 1.

[639] *Re Freudiana Holdings Ltd, Times, 4 December 1995.* Thus solicitors were not ordered to show cause in *Kagalovsky v Balmore Invest Ltd* [2015] EWHC 1337 (QB); [2015] P.N.L.R 26, where the allegations concerned participation in the client's fraud, and involved a variety of allegations and volume of material concerning matters which did not occur in the face of the court.

[640] *Manzanilla Ltd v Corton Property and Investments Ltd* [1997] 3 F.C.R. 389.

[641] *Turner Page Music Ltd v Torres Design Associates Ltd, Times* 7 August 1998. For an example see *Lakatamia Shipping Co Ltd v Baker McKenzie LLP* [2021] EWHC 2702 (Comm); [2021] Costs L.R. 1187, where the applicant at stage one showed that on some of the allegations made there was material which, if unanswered, would lead to a finding of improper, unreasonable or negligent conduct. However, on none of them was causation likely to be shown, and the fact that it would take a two-day hearing and many hundreds of thousands of pounds of costs at stage two meant that the application should not be permitted to proceed.

[642] *Wall v Lefever* [1998] 1 F.C.R. 605. In *Chief Constable of North Yorkshire v Audsley* [2000] Lloyd's Rep. P.N. 675 QBD, the likely costs of the wasted costs hearing was disproportionate and was therefore not pursued. For an example of a case where more time was spent on the wasted costs hearing than the substantive proceedings, see *Re Merc Property Ltd, Times,* 19 May 1999, Ch. D.

[643] *Royal Institution of Chartered Surveyors v Wiseman Marshall* [2000] P.N.L.R. 649.

[644] [2001] UKPC 18; [2001] 2 A.C. 678; see further para.12-019. Turner J refused to allow a wasted costs application to proceed even to the first stage in *B v Pendelbury* [2002] EWHC 1797; [2003] P.N.L.R. 1, because there was substantial dispute on the facts, and the allegations which were based on impropriety and fraud were unsuitable to be determined in a summary jurisdiction.

[645] [2003] EWCA Civ 469; [2003] P.N.L.R. 29.

Hopeless litigation

Replace footnote 667 with:

⁶⁶⁷ [1996] 1 W.L.R. 491. Similarly, in *Re A Company (No. 0022 of 1993)* [1993] B.C.C. 726, Knox J **11-138** held solicitors liable for wasted costs after they should have realised that an attempt to wind up a company was inappropriate because it was clear that the debt was disputed. In *Isaacs Partnership (A Firm) v Umm Al-Jawaby Oil Service Co Ltd (Wasted Costs)* [2003] EWHC 2539 (QB); [2004] P.N.L.R. 9, a wasted costs order was upheld by Gross J against solicitors who had pursued hopeless litigation against the wrong defendant for breach of an employment contract, when they had both documentary evidence and a letter from the defendants pointing out that the claimant had been employed by another company. Wasted cost orders were made by Henrique J in *Secretary of State for the Home Department v Zinovjev (Wasted Costs Order)* [2003] EWHC 100 (Admin); [2004] P.N.L.R. 4 in four immigration appeals, all abandoned on the day of the appeal, where the appeal was made out of time without any explanation and on formulaic and unfocused grounds. In *R. (on the application of Gassama) v Secretary of State for the Home Department* [2012] EWHC 3049 (Admin); [2013] P.N.L.R. 10, the solicitors made an application for judicial review claiming that their client should have indefinite leave to remain in the UK. The claim was stayed pending other litigation which, when decided, was very unfavourable to the claimant, as the Treasury Solicitor pointed out to the solicitors, who withdrew the claim only two days before the hearing, and a wasted costs order was made against them. A wasted costs order was upheld in *Thames Chambers Solicitors v Miah* [2013] EWHC 1245 (QB); [2013] P.N.L.R. 30 where the solicitors acted for a client whom they knew was bankrupt, and they should have realised that the bankrupt's assets were vested in his trustee in bankruptcy. Similarly, in *Rushbrooke UK Ltd v 4 Designs Concept Ltd* [2022] EWHC 1687 (Ch); [2022] Costs L.R. 1083 solicitors purported to act for a company in an application to restrain the presentation of a winding up petition, and they failed to consider whether the director who had instructed them had authority to do so when there was deadlock between the directors.

(g) Practice and Procedure

(ii) Privilege

Two clients

Replace footnote 732 with:

⁷³² For a detailed treatment of disclosure and privilege, W. Flenley, T. Leech and others in *The Law of* **11-151** *Solicitors' Negligence and Liability*, 4th edn (London: Bloomsbury Professional, 2020), Ch.14.

(h) Authority, Attribution and Vicarious Liability

Authority from the client

Replace footnote 740 with:

⁷⁴⁰ [2002] EWCA Civ 253; [2002] P.N.L.R. 26. The case was applied by Cooke J in *Euroafrica Ship-* **11-152** *ping Lines Co Ltd v Zeguila Polska SA* [2004] EWHC 385 (Comm); [2004] 2 B.C.L.C. 97, where there were difficulties in obtaining instructions as there was a dispute about the constitution of the client company. See also *Rushbrooke UK Ltd v 4 Designs Concept Ltd* [2022] EWHC 1687 (Ch); [2022] Costs L.R. 1083 where solicitors purported to act for a company in an application to restrain the presentation of a winding up petition, but failed to consider whether the director who had instructed them had authority to do so when there was deadlock between the directors. The solicitors were held liable for wasted costs.

3. DAMAGES

(b) Claims at Common Law: Causation, Duty Nexus and Legal Responsibility for Loss

Replace footnote 1174 with:

¹¹⁷⁴ [2021] UKSC 20; [2022] A.C. 783 and in particular [6].   **11-251**

(i) Factual causation

"But for" causation

Replace footnote 1175 with:

11-252   ¹¹⁷⁵ For a statement of the general principles, see J. Edelman and others (eds), *McGregor on Damages*, 21st edn (London: Sweet & Maxwell, 2021), Ch.8, paras 8-003 to 8-056 (in relation to tort) and paras 8-140 to 8-144 (in relation to contract). See also *Manchester Building Society v Grant Thornton UK LLP* [2021] UKSC 20; [2022] A.C. 783 at [6(3)].

The cause of or the occasion of the loss

Replace paragraph 11-253 (to incorporate updates to footnotes 1185 and 1191) with:

11-253   An early case exploring the need for a sufficient link between the defendant's breach of duty and the loss was the accountant's negligence case of *Galoo Ltd v Bright Grahame Murray*.¹¹⁸⁴ This held that that a distinction must be drawn between a breach which gives the "occasion" for the loss and one which is the substantial "cause" of the loss.¹¹⁸⁵ The *Galoo* approach was applied in the solicitors' case of *Young v Purdy*.¹¹⁸⁶ There, solicitors wrongfully terminated a retainer to act for the plaintiff in proceedings for ancillary relief. She continued to act for herself, and by remarrying she effectively lost the right to claim relief. The Court of Appeal concluded that the solicitor's negligence was the occasion and not the cause of the loss as the plaintiff acted negligently, and they also held that the loss was not foreseeable. However, in *Aneco Ltd v Johnson Higgins Ltd*.¹¹⁸⁷ Evans LJ suggested that the search for an effective cause had been replaced by an inquiry into the scope of the duty of care, following *South Australia Asset Management Corp v York Montague Ltd*,¹¹⁸⁸ (a decision usually referred to as *SAAMCO*).¹¹⁸⁹ That approach has subsequently been endorsed by the Supreme Court in *Manchester Building Society v Grant Thornton UK LLP*.¹¹⁹⁰ The focus is therefore now on identifying a nexus between the scope of duty and the loss claimed.¹¹⁹¹

¹¹⁸⁴ [1994] 1 W.L.R. 1360 CA, on which see para.17-129, and see *Bernasconi v Nicholas Bennett* [2000] Lloyd's Rep. P.N. 285, discussed in para.12-044. See also *MacMahon v James Doran & Co* [2002] P.N.L.R. 33 where the plaintiff ran up a sizeable overdraft as a result of the defendant's solicitors delaying litigation on his behalf. Relying on *Galoo*, the Northern Ireland Court of Appeal held that the solicitors were not liable for the overdraft because the incurring of a capital obligation to repay was not a loss as it was balanced by the receipt of the sum advanced. The claimant could recover the interest payments.

¹¹⁸⁵ The case has more recently been explained as a manifestation of the principle that loss must fall within the scope of a defendant's duty. In *Manchester Building Society v Grant Thornton UK LLP* [2021] UKSC 20; [2022] A.C. 783, Lord Leggatt at [118] stated that "in order to show that the losses suffered by the companies in continuing to trade were losses which the auditors owed a duty to protect the companies against, it would have been necessary to plead and prove the existence of a causal link between the losses and those matters which the auditors negligently failed to detect".

¹¹⁸⁶ [1997] P.N.L.R. 130. cf. *Redbus LMDS Ltd v Jeffrey Green & Russell (A Firm)* [2007] EWHC 2938 (Ch); [2007] P.N.L.R. 12, where it was held that a solicitor's negligence, in failing to make clear in drafting articles of association of a company that sub-licences of a licence which it owned could be granted without consent, was the effective cause of subsequent litigation costs between the two groups which controlled the company, as it allowed arguments to be run regarding the wording of the licence. See also *British Racing Drivers Club v Hextall Erskine & Co (A Firm)* [1996] 4 All E.R. 667, discussed at para.11-262.

¹¹⁸⁷ [2000] P.N.L.R. 152 at 161C, an insurers brokers' case, on which see see paras 16-178 to 16-179.

¹¹⁸⁸ [1997] 1 A.C. 191.

¹¹⁸⁹ [1997] A.C. 191. For the law on scope of duty see paras 11-254 onwards.

¹¹⁹⁰ [2021] UKSC 20; [2022] A.C. 783 at [6(d)] and [8].

[1191] See paras 2-143 onwards; H. Evans, "The scope of the duty revisited" (2001) 17 P.N. 146; Evans, *Lawyers' Liabilities* (2002), Ch.9 and L. Hoffmann "Causation" (2005) 121 L.Q.R. 593.

(ii) The duty nexus and scope of duty

Replace footnote 1192 with:

[1192] [2021] UKSC 20; [2022] A.C. 783 at [6(d)] and [8].   **11-254**

The origins of the duty nexus principle

SAAMCO

Replace footnote 1196 with:

[1196] In this regard the scope of the duty is governed by the purpose of the advice being given, objectively   **11-255**
construed, which is the risk the duty was supposed to guard against, as emphasised in *Manchester Building Society v Grant Thornton UK LLP* [2021] UKSC 20; [2022] A.C. 783 at [13]–[17].

Replace footnote 1201 with:

[1201] [2021] UKSC 20; [2022] A.C. 783, see paras 17-136 onwards. The scope of duty issue should be considered as part of six general questions, see [6]: actionability; scope of duty; breach; factual causation; duty nexus; and legal responsibility. This case also doubted the appropriateness of the "information" and "advice" distinction which many previous authorities had derived from *SAAMCO*.

Hughes-Holland v BPE Solicitors

Replace footnote 1203 with:

[1203] Note the disapproval of the distinction between "information" and "advice" cases in *Manchester*   **11-256**
Building Society v Grant Thornton UK LLP [2021] UKSC 20; [2022] A.C. 783 at [22]. There, the Supreme Court pointed out the shortcomings of the "information" and "advice" labels. Instead, it held that the focus should be on the purpose of the duty assumed.

Replace paragraph 11-257 (to incorporate updates to footnotes 1204 and 1206) with:

Four points from the judgment of Lord Sumption are particularly important   **11-257**
(although some of the terminology adopted, and in particular the distinction drawn between "information" and "advice" cases has to be treated with caution in view of *Manchester Building Society v Grant Thornton UK LLP*).[1204] First, a valuer or a conveyancer will rarely supply more a limited part of the material on which the client will rely in deciding to enter a transaction from those where he has a duty to consider all relevant matters in deciding whether the client should do so. In this regard, the fact that the professional's advice is critical does not render the professional liable for all of the consequences of entering into a transaction. Secondly, if the information which has not been provided would have shown that the transaction was not viable, or reveals an actual or potential fraud, then this does not make the professional liable for all of the consequences of entering into the transaction (and the Supreme Court overruled a previous line of cases in this regard[1205]). Thirdly, Lord Sumption approved Lord Hoffmann's principle in *SAAMCO* that a professional is not responsible for losses which would have occurred even if the information provided by the professional had been correct,[1206] adding that the maximum measure of the professional's liability is the increased risk to which he exposed the client. Fourthly, the claimant must plead and has the burden of proof in showing what loss was within the scope of the defendant professional's duty.[1207]

[1204] [2021] UKSC 20; [2022] A.C. 783 at [22].

[1205] The cases that were overruled included *Portman Building Society v Bevan Ashford (A Firm)* [2000]

P.N.L.R. 344. There, a solicitor had failed to report matters relating to the borrower's financial condition to the lender and was liable for the whole lost. The Court of Appeal stated: "… where a negligent solicitor fails to provide information which shows that the transaction is not viable or which tends to reveal an actual or potential fraud on the part of the borrowers, the lender is entitled to recover the whole of its loss". The Supreme Court also overruled the *Steggles Palmer* case in *Bristol & West Building Society v Fancy & Jackson (A Firm)* [1997] 4 All E.R. 582.

1206 Lord Sumption described this "counterfactual" (i.e. the examination of what would have happened if the solicitors had been right) as a tool. In *Manchester Building Society v Grant Thornton UK LLP* [2021] UKSC 20; [2022] A.C. 783 at [33] the Supreme Court described the consideration of a counterfactual as a useful cross-check in most cases, but cautioned that it did not replace the primary issue of an analysis of the scope of the duty.

1207 For commentary, see H. Evans: "Solicitors and the scope of duty in the Supreme Court" (2017) 33 P.N. 193; D. Ryan "SAAMCO re-explored: BPE and the law of professional negligence" (2018) 34 P.N. 71; and J. Thomson: "SAMCO revisited" [2017] C.L.J. 476.

Manchester Building Society v Grant Thornton UK LLP

Replace paragraph 11-258 (to incorporate updates to footnotes 1208 and 1209) with:

11-258 The Supreme Court case of *Manchester Building Society v Grant Thornton UK LLP*1208 makes clear that the distinction often drawn between "information" and "advice" cases should not be treated as a "straitjacket" and has proven unsatisfactory.1209 It also holds that rather than focusing on categorising the key issue for the court to consider is the scope or purpose of the solicitors' duty, and whether there is a sufficient nexus between the loss and the defendant's duty of care. Finally, it makes clear that the use of "counterfactual analysis"1210 should only be a tool to cross check the result reached pursuant to the analysis of the purpose of a professional's duty.

1208 [2021] UKSC 20; [2022] A.C. 783; see paras 17-136 onwards. The scope of duty issue should be considered as part of six general questions, see [6]: actionability; scope of duty; breach; factual causation; duty nexus; and legal responsibility.

1209 [2021] UKSC 20; [2022] A.C. 783 at [4] and [18].

1210 i.e. considering what the position would have been if the defendant's negligent information or advice had in fact been correct.

Liability for commercial losses?

Replace footnote 1219 with:

11-260 1219 [2021] UKSC 20; [2022] A.C. 783; see paras 17-136 onwards.

(iii) Legal Responsibility

Intervening act of the claimant

Replace paragraph 11-261 (to incorporate updates to footnotes 1222 and 1225) with:

11-261 After other issues of causation and the duty nexus have been considered, the court must turn to the "legal responsibility question". This includes whether the harm for which the claimant seeks damages is irrecoverable because it is too remote, or because there is another effective cause (such as the intervening act of someone other than the defendant), or the claimant has mitigated his loss or failed to do so,1221 see *Manchester Building Society v Grant Thornton UK LLP*.1222 One such issue is whether the immediate cause of the damage in question was some unwise action or inaction on the part of the claimant, and if so the court may hold that the chain of causation has been broken. A number of cases illustrate this principle.[1223] In *Simmons v Pennington*,[1224] the plaintiff, on the advice of his solicitors, decided not to resell his property, pending the outcome of certain litigation. During this period the property was damaged by fire and, since the insurance policy had lapsed, the plaintiff suffered loss. The Court of Appeal held that it was not necessary to determine whether the solicitor's advice was negligent, since the damages claimed were too remote.[1225] The plaintiff's loss was due to his own failure to insure.[1226] It was also held that the damage was not foreseeable. In *Joyce v Darby & Darby*,[1227] the defendant solicitors negligently failed to inform the claimant that property she was buying was affected by a restrictive covenant requiring the consent of neighbours to external alterations. When she undertook such works, the neighbours objected, and the defendant advised her to stop work and reach agreement, or she would be sued. The claimant then carried out further work, and became involved in injunction proceedings, but the costs of them were not recoverable from the defendants.

[1221] See paras 11-342 onwards in relation to mitigation; the other issues are considered in this section.

[1222] [2021] UKSC 20; [2022] A.C. 783 at [6].

[1223] See also *Frank v Seifert Sedley & Co* (1964) 108 S.J. 523, QBD. On the purchase of a lease the solicitors' negligence caused an increase in purchase price of £1,500, but no loss was caused as the plaintiff failed to complete despite being able to raise the money to pay the increased purchase price. In *Mallesons Stephen Jaques v Trenorth Ltd* [1999] 1 V.R. 727 Victoria CA, the defendant solicitors acted for the vendors of commercial premises. They were negligent in failing to include in their draft disclosure statement reference to a supplemental agreement with the tenant giving him a rent-free period. However, there was a break in the chain of causation by the vendor's fraudulent nondisclosure of that agreement to the purchaser. In *Hudson v Atanskovic* [2014] NSWCA 255; (2015) 311 A.L.R. 290, solicitors drafted a contract which provided that the claimant would be paid by the other contracting party selling the whole of certain land, which was allegedly negligent, but it also included a provision for the claimant to prevent sale of part of that land, which the claimant failed to invoke on such partial sale, and any negligence by the solicitors therefore did not cause the loss of the payment. In contrast, solicitors drafted an illegal lease for the tenant in *Mackinlay v Derry Dew Pty Ltd* [2014] WASCA 24; (2014) 46 W.A.R. 247, and after later negotiations with the landlord had failed, the tenant terminated it is occupancy of the land. That termination was not unreasonable, as the tenant did not have a saleable asset. For another case where there was no finding of a break in the chain of causation see *Vision Golf Ltd v Weightmans (A Firm)* [2005] EWHC 1675 (Ch); [2006] 1 P. & C.R. DG13 in which the defendants breached their duty in failing to apply to the court on behalf of their tenant clients for relief from forfeiture. This application would have succeeded, and the defendants argued that this caused no loss because an application for relief by new solicitors would also have succeeded. Lewison J dismissed this argument. The loss would have been avoided if the defendants had acted as they should have. There was no claim that the subsequent solicitors had acted unreasonably, and thus it was irrelevant that a subsequent application may have succeeded, although the judge also held that it would have been a difficult one to make. For the decision on the assessment of damages see [2006] EWHC 1766 (Ch); [2007] P.N.L.R. 8.

[1224] [1955] 1 W.L.R. 183.

[1225] This does not accord with the structure of the questions posed at [6] of *Manchester Building Society v Grant Thornton UK LLP* [2021] UKSC 20; [2022] A.C. 783.

[1226] per Denning LJ. See also *Clark v Kirby-Smith* [1964] 1 Ch. 506, where the plaintiffs lost the opportunity to renew their lease of business premises as a result of their solicitors' negligence. On leaving the premises they were faced with a claim by their landlords for dilapidations, which they settled for £120. Plowman J held that this loss was not caused by the solicitors' negligence, but by the plaintiffs' own breach of covenant.

[1227] [2014] EWCA Civ 677; [2014] 3 E.G.L.R. 49.

Foreseeability: general rules as a result of Wellesley

Replace footnote 1235 with:

[1235] For a full discussion of the requirement of foreseeability in tort, see *McGregor on Damages* (2021, **11-264**

[81]

1st supp, 2021), Ch.8, paras 8-057 to 8-139. In *Cadoks Pty Ltd v Wallace Westley & Vigar Pty Ltd* [2000] VSC 167; (2000) 2 V.R. 569 Victoria Supreme Court, the loss was foreseeable in tort, but not contract. The defendant solicitors negligently failed to ensure their clients had finance in place for the purchase of a farm, causing a delay in purchase of 15 months. The solicitors knew that the plaintiff intended to resell, but the loss of the opportunity to sell at a favourable time was held to be too remote in contract although not in tort.

(d)   Heads of Damage

(v)   *Losses on Loans Secured by Mortgages*

Scope of duty

Replace paragraph 11-322 (to incorporate updates to footnotes 1461 and 1465) with:

11-322   The measures of loss discussed in the previous paragraph will be further subject to the principle in *South Australia Asset Management Corp v York Montague Ltd* (also known as *SAAMCO*).[1460] There, the House of Lords held that someone under a duty to advise on the appropriate course of action will be liable for all the foreseeable consequences of the action taken in reliance, but a person under a duty to take reasonable care to provide information on which someone relies will generally be regarded as responsible for the consequences of the information being wrong, and not all the consequences of the reliance[1461]. Thus surveyors sued by lenders were only responsible for the losses sustained up to the difference between the correct valuation and their negligent valuation. In *Bristol & West Building Society v Mothew*,[1462] the Court of Appeal applied this principle to a case where the defendant solicitors had misrepresented to the plaintiff lender that the borrower had no other indebtedness. While the plaintiff's loss from the loan was large, the loss within the scope of the broken duty appeared to be modest, as the small size of the borrower's liability may have had a minimal or no effect on their ability to make mortgage repayments to the plaintiff. Determination of the size of the loss was left to the assessment of damages. While a solicitor's duty will be wider than that of a valuer, *Mothew* supports the view that there is no wide duty to advise on the appropriate course of action.[1463] There used to be an exception so that the whole loss could be recovered in cases where a negligent solicitor failed to provide information which showed that the transaction was not viable or which tended to reveal an actual or potential fraud on the part of the borrowers, but this has been overruled by the Supreme Court in *Hughes-Holland v BPE Solicitors*.[1464] Furthermore, the formulaic distinction between "information" and "advice" cases has recently been disapproved by the Supreme Court in *Manchester Building Society v Grant Thornton UK LLP*, which makes clear that the crucial issue is whether there is sufficient nexus between the loss and the scope of the defendant's duty.[1465]

[1460] [1997] A.C. 191, see para.11-254 onwards. For a further explanation of how the principle works in the context of awarding interest, see *Nykredit Mortgage Bank Plc v Edward Erdman Group Ltd (No.2)* [1997] 1 W.L.R. 1627, considered in para.10-215. For the effect of contributory negligence on a claim which is subject to a limit from the scope of the duty owed, see *Platform Home Loans Ltd v Oyston Shipways Ltd* [2000] 2 A.C. 190 (contributory negligence generally only deducted from the whole loss), considered in paras 10-248 onwards.

[1461] Note that the formulaic distinction between "information" and "advice" cases derived from *SAAMCO* was disapproved by the Supreme Court in *Manchester Building Society v Grant Thornton UK LLP* [2021] UKSC 20; [2022] A.C. 783 at [22].

[1462] [1996] 4 All E.R. 698. See also *The Mortgage Corp v Tisdall Nelson Nari & Co* [1998] P.N.L.R. 81 QBD, which applied *South Australia Asset Management Corp v York Montague Ltd (SAAMCO)* to limit damages, and *Halifax Building Society v Richard Grosse & Co* [1997] E.G.C.S. 111. In *Broker House Insurance Services Ltd v OJS Law* [2010] EWHC 3816 (Ch); [2011] P.N.L.R. 23, solicitors failed to obtain the consent of the first legal chargeholder to a second charge, or to register it, but were held not liable for the borrower's inability to repay or subsequent falls in the market.

[1463] cf. the position in Scotland where it was held in *Bristol & West Building Society v Rollo Steven Bond* 1998 S.L.T. 9, that the solicitors effectively advised the building society to take a certain course of action and were responsible for the full loss. Similarly, in *Leeds Holbeck Building Society v Alex Morison Co (No.2)* [2001] P.N.L.R. 13, where it was held that if the defenders had been negligent in failing to report that the borrowers intended in due course to use the property for business purposes, then they would have been liable for the full losses as the matter was relevant to the risk of default. See to similar effect *Newcastle Building Society v Paterson Robertson & Graham* [2001] P.N.L.R. 780 and 2002 S.L.T. 177, where the alleged errors went to the heart of the transaction, and *Preferred Mortgages Ltd v Shanks* [2008] CSOH 23; [2008] P.N.L.R. 20, where solicitors failed to advise that title to property was seriously defective. Similarly, in the Irish case of *KBC Bank v BCM Hanby Wallace* [2012] IEHC 120; [2013] P.N.L.R. 7, the solicitors had misled the bank about the availability of the security properties, and were liable for the whole loss, and not just the value of the expected securities. While there was a successful appeal on whether the solicitors had acted dishonestly, there was no challenge to this conclusion on appeal at [2013] IESC 32; [2013] P.N.L.R. 33.

[1464] [2017] UKSC 21; [2018] A.C. 599 at [50]–[52], expressly overruling the *Steggles Palmer* case in *Bristol & West Building Society v Fancy & Jackson (A Firm)*, [1997] 4 All E.R. 582, and *Portman Building Society v Bevan Ashford (A Firm)* [2000] P.N.L.R. 344 at 359, and although not expressly mentioned also *Nationwide Building Society v JR Jones* [1999] Lloyd's Rep. P.N. 414 and *Lloyds Bank Plc v Crosse & Crosse* [2001] P.N.L.R. 34.

[1465] [2021] UKSC 20; [2022] A.C. 783 at [6] and [22].

(viii)   Criminal Liability

Replace footnote 1488 with:

[1488] *Osman v J Ralph Moss* [1970] 1 Lloyd's Rep. 313. In other cases, considerations of public policy **11-331** preclude the recovery of any damages. For a general discussion of this topic, see *McGregor on Damages* (2021, 1st supp, 2021), Ch.12, paras 12-069 onwards.

(ix)   Wasted Expenditure

Later solicitor's costs

Replace footnote 1503 with:

[1503] [1996] 3 All E.R. 667, Carnwarth J. For the facts see para.11-262. For another example, see *Savoie* **11-335** *v Mailhot* 2004 NBCA 17; (2004) 268 N.B.R. (2d) 348, NBCA. The defendant solicitors' failure to describe the property properly in a deed of sale led to successful litigation by the plaintiff, who was unable to enforce his costs order and recovered those costs from the defendant solicitors. For a more detailed treatment of whether costs should be recovered on an indemnity or standard basis see *McGregor on Damages* (2021, 1st supp, 2021), Ch.21, paras 21-003 to 21-011, where it is argued that old authority permitting recovery on an indemnity basis should be preferred.

CHAPTER 12

BARRISTERS

1. GENERAL

(b) Duties to the Clients

Tort and other duties

Replace footnote 23 with:

[23] *R. v Blatt, Times* 30 May 1996. In *Geveran Trading Co Ltd v Skjevesland* [2002] EWCA Civ 1567; **12-005**
[2003] 1 W.L.R. 912, the Court of Appeal held that in exceptional circumstances the court could prevent
an advocate from acting even where he did not possess confidential information if satisfied that there
was a real risk that his continued participation would require the order made at trial to be set aside on
appeal. Such an order was made in *Ahmed v Iqbal* [2020] EWHC 2666 (Fam); [2021] 2 F.C.R.1.

(f) Abuse of Process

Replace paragraph 12-012 (to incorporate new text and footnote) with:

In *Hall v Simons*[55] the House of Lords held that the abuse of process principle **12-012**
would ordinarily prevent a claimant suing for a wrongful criminal conviction, as it
would be a collateral attack on the verdict of the criminal trial, but that in civil actions that principle will rarely have a place.[56] Abuse of process was held not to be
relevant in *Percy v Merriman White (A Firm)*.[56a] There, a client was in dispute with
his business partner with whom he had set up a joint venture company. The barrister advised the client to commence a derivative claim, but the Court refused
permission for it. In contribution proceedings brought by the solicitors against the
barrister, the Court of Appeal held that the barrister was entitled to allege that the

judge's decision refusing permission was wrong or that other judges may have reached a different decision. The barrister had not been a party to that decision and there had been no judgment against him.

[55] [2002] 1 A.C. 615.

[56] This issue is discussed in paras 11-113 onwards.

[56a] [2022] EWCA Civ 493; [2022] 3 W.L.R. 1.

2. LIABILITY FOR BREACH OF DUTY

Add new heading footnote 130a:

Settlement[130a]

12-032   [130a] A barrister will generally have ostensible authority to agree a settlement, although consent can be withdrawn if no consent was given by the client if a consent order has not been drawn up: *Ashford BC v Wilson* [2022] EWHC 988 (QB); [2022] Costs L.R. 949.

4. SHARED RESPONSIBILITY

(a) Apportionment of Liability

Replace paragraph 12-046 (to incorporate updates to footnotes and deletion of text and footnote 181) with:

12-046   Apportionment between solicitors and barristers has arisen in a number of cases. There may be technical difficulties preventing contribution proceedings in wasted costs cases[177]; the wasted costs application sometimes being made against both solicitors and counsel, and the court then having to determine what proportion of the costs each will pay. In a number of wasted costs applications, a division between the barrister and the solicitor was determined at 75/25,[178] but each case will depend on its own facts.[179] In *Hickman v Blake Lapthorn*,[180] negligent advice was given on settlement at the start of a trial on liability, which did not take into account the prospects of the claimant not working again. The barrister, who was a senior junior, had a leading role in valuing the claim and advising on settlement, but the solicitor had a greater knowledge of quantum. Responsibility was apportioned two-thirds to one-third.

[177] See H. Evans, "The wasted costs jurisdiction" (2001) 64 M.L.R. 51, 60–62.

[178] *R. v Secretary of State of the Home Department Ex p. Begum* [1995] COD 176, Harrison J, where the solicitors wrongly relied on counsel's opinion in a judicial review application. *B v B (Wasted Costs: Abuse of Process)* [2001] 1 F.L.R. 843, Wall J where an order vacating a trial date had been hopelessly appealed; the directions which were given, and which were not appealed made it inevitable that the hearing would be postponed. See also *Moy v Pettman Smith (A Firm)* [2002] EWCA Civ 875; [2002] P.N.L.R. 44. The Court of Appeal held that the solicitor, who failed to obtain a proper report on causation in a clinical negligence case, was 75% to blame. The barrister failed to inform her client of her assessment of the chances of the court permitting him to adduce late evidence on causation, as a result of which he turned down an offer of about half the value of the claim; she was found to be responsible for 25% of the loss. On appeal, the House of Lords held that the barrister was not negligent, see [2005] UKHL 7; [2005] 1 W.L.R. 581. Similarly, in *Prichard Joyce & Hinds (A Firm) v Batcup* [2008] EWHC 20 (QB); [2008] P.N.L.R. 18, where in an ordinary claim rather than a wasted costs application Underhill J ordered leading and junior counsel to pay a 75% contribution, because their relationship was of the conventional kind where solicitors looked to counsel for authoritative guidance on the major strategic questions in litigation. The barristers were held not to be liable on appeal, [2009] EWCA Civ 369; [2009] P.N.L.R. 28. In *Percy v Merriman White (A Firm)* [2021] EWHC 22 (Ch); [2021] P.N.L.R. 11 responsibility was allocated 60% to the solicitor who was responsible for advising the client to reject an attractive offer at mediation (although the barrister later failed to advise that the offer should be

revisited), and 40% to the barrister who was primarily responsible for advising a derivative action for which permission was then refused. However, the decision was overturned on appeal, [2022] EWCA Civ 493;[2022] 3 W.L.R. 1. The Civil Liability (Contribution) Act 1978 s.1(4) did not have the effect that the solicitors did not have to prove the client's claim against the barrister, and they had failed to prove that the barrister was negligent or caused loss. Further, it was not involve an abusive collateral attack for the barrister to argue that a different judge may have reached a different view on whether a derivative action was appropriate.

[179] In *McFaddens (A Firm) v Platford* [2009] EWHC 126 (TCC); [2009] P.N.L.R. 26 the defendant barrister was found not to be negligent, but if he had been the division of responsibility would have been 75% to the solicitors and 25% to the barrister.

[180] [2005] EWHC 2714; [2006] P.N.L.R. 20. In *Bray v Dye (No.2)* [2010] VSC 152; (2010) 27 V.R. 324, Judd J held that there was an equal division of fault between barrister and solicitor for acting for the second plaintiff who had not authorised proceedings. The barrister had introduced the first plaintiff to the solicitor, and both lawyers had failed to make adequate enquiries with the second plaintiff. Quaere whether the barrister would be held liable in this jurisdiction.

CHAPTER 13

MEDICAL PRACTITIONERS

1. INTRODUCTION

Replace paragraph 13-001 (to incorporate text and footnote updates) with:

13-001   This chapter is confined to a short overview of professional liability law as it relates to medical practitioners. The number of practitioner-authors with significant experience of clinical liability is relatively limited. Given that the general principles to be applied are, or at least should be, the same as a number of the other registered professions, it is often of importance to understand the application of such principles in different areas. While relevant case law mainly relates to doctors, the chapter also features cases as they apply to other medical professions, such as dentistry. For a fuller treatment of professional liability law as it relates to medical practitioners, reference should be made to specialist works.[1]

[1] Notable works in the field include A. Buchan and others (eds), *Lewis and Buchan: Clinical Negligence: A Practical Guide*, 8th edn (London: Bloomsbury Professional, 2019); D. Gomez and others (eds), *The Regulation of Healthcare Professionals: Law, Principle and Process*, 2nd edn (London: Sweet & Maxwell, 2019); M.A. Jones, *Medical Negligence*, 6th edn (London: Sweet & Maxwell, 2021); J. Whitfield, G. Hobcraft and others (eds), *Professional Discipline and Healthcare Regulators: A Legal Handbook*, 2nd edn (London: Legal Action Group, 2018); J. Laing, J. McHale, Sir Ian Kennedy, A. Grubb and others (eds), *Principles of Medical Law*, 4th edn (Oxford: Oxford University Press, 2017), and M. Powers and A. Barton, *Clinical Negligence*, 5th edn (London: Bloomsbury Professional, 2015) (6th edn, forthcoming, 2023). The following works also contain a chapter on the healthcare profession and clinical practitioners: Dame Alison Foster, G. Treverton-Jones, and S. Hanif, *Disciplinary and Regulatory Proceedings*, 10th edn (London: LexisNexis 2019), Ch.13 (on healthcare) and M. Simpson and others (eds), *Professional Negligence and Liability*, Issue 41 (London: Informa, 2022), Ch.14 (on clinical practitioners). More broadly, see too S. Pattinson, *Medical Law and Ethics*, 6th edn (London: Sweet & Maxwell, 2020), J. Herring, *Medical Law and Ethics*, 9th edn (Oxford: Oxford University Press, 2022) and G. T. Laurie, S. H. E. Harmon, E. S. Dove (eds), *Mason and McCall Smith's Law and Medical Ethics*, 11th edn (Oxford: Oxford University Press, 2019).

2. DUTIES

(a)   The Regulatory Framework

13-003 *In paragraph 13-003, after "is pending; place", delete "on".*

(c)   Duties to Third Parties

Replace footnote 37 with:

13-015 [37] See *McLoughlin v O'Brian* [1983] 1 A.C. 410; *Alcock v Chief Constable of South Yorkshire Police* [1992] 1 A.C. 310 HL; *Frost v Chief Constable of South Yorkshire Police* [1999] 2 A.C. 455 HL. For a full discussion of liability for psychiatric injury and distress, including the important distinction between "primary" and "secondary" victims see M.A. Jones, A. Dugdale and others (eds), *Clerk & Lindsell on Torts*, 23rd edn (London: Sweet & Maxwell, 2020, 2nd supp, 2022), Ch.8, paras 8–63 to 8–79. See also *Taylor v A Novo (UK) Ltd* [2013] EWCA Civ 194; [2014] Q.B. 150. It was applied in *RS v Criminal Injuries Compensation Authority* [2013] EWCA Civ 1040; [2014] 1 W.L.R. 1313, which concerned the proper interpretation of para.9(b)(ii) of the Criminal Injuries Compensation Scheme 2008.

(d)   The Standard of Skill and Care

(ii)   The Advisory Role

Materiality of risk

Replace footnote 56 with:

[56] There is a prior stage. See *Duce v Worcestershire Acute Hospitals NHS Trust* [2018] EWCA Civ 1307; [2018] P.I.Q.R. P18 ([30]–[42]) in which the Court of Appeal found that whilst the judge at first instance had correctly considered *Montgomery*, he had not needed to address the issue of materiality because he had found that the claim failed at the first hurdle, i.e. there was no proof that the medic was or should have been aware of the relevant risks. See here *Ollosson v Lee* [2019] EWHC 784 (QB), in which *Duce* was applied and Mr Justice Stewart held, on behalf of the Queen's Bench Division: "The quantification of the risk is a matter for the experts. What should be told to a patient is a matter for the court." at [153].   **13-023**

(iii)   Diagnosis and treatment roles

Replace heading footnote 85 with:

Res ipsa loquitur[85]

[85] For a classic statement, see Erle CJ in *Scott v London & St Katherine Docks* (1865) 3 H. & C. 596 at 601: "There must be reasonable evidence of negligence. But where *the thing* is shown to be under the management of the defendant or his servants, and the accident is such as in the ordinary course of things does not happen if those who have the management use proper care, it affords reasonable evidence, in the absence of explanation by the defendants, that the accident arose from want of care." The facts were that three bags of sugar fell from an upper storey of a warehouse on to the claimant. This raised a presumption of negligence on the part of those in control of the sugar. For a full exposition of the maxim, see *Clerk & Lindsell on Torts* (2020, 2nd supp, 2022), Ch.8, paras 8-184 to 8-188.   **13-035**

(e)   Consent to Treatment

(iv)   Capacity to Consent

Emergency

Replace footnote 104 with:

[104] See *Re F (Mental Patient: Sterilisation)* [1990] 2 A.C. 1 at 55 per Lord Brandon and at 712–778 per Lord Goff. Further, in relation to the issues raised in para.13-045 and associated sections in this chapter, see too *Parfitt v Guy's and St Thomas' Children's NHS Foundation Trust* [2021] EWCA Civ 362; [2021] 5 Med. L. R. 323 (Lord Justice Baker), in which *Re F* was followed.   **13-045**

Withdrawal of treatment from insensate patients

Replace paragraph 13-049 (to incorporate updates to text and footnote 119) with:

A medical practitioner is under no duty to provide medical treatment and care to a patient who is unable to benefit from it.[117] The *Bolam* test applies to determine whether treatment and care is beneficial to, or in the best interests of, a patient who is unable to consent to their discontinuance.[118] As to whether to withdraw treatment from a critically ill patient lacking capacity, including children, the focus should be on whether it is in the patient's best interests to give the treatment, rather than on whether it is in his best interests to withhold or withdraw it.[119] When considering the best interests of a patient at a particular time, decision-makers must look at his welfare in the widest sense.[120]   **13-049**

[117] *Airedale NHS Trust v Bland* [1993] A.C. 789, applying the principles in *Re F* [1990] 2 A.C. 1. The case concerned a patient who was in a persistent vegetative state from which he would not recover.

[118] ibid. at 362E, 373D–373E and at 385F–385Gn. *Airedale* was distinguished in *SL (Adult Patient: Sterilisations: Patient's Best Interests)* [2001] Fam. 15 CA. See also *R. (on the application of Burke) v General Medical Council* [2004] EWHC 1879 (Admin); [2005] Q.B. 424 and on appeal [2005] EWCA Civ 1003; [2006] Q.B. 273; and *AVS v NHS Foundation Trust* [2011] EWCA Civ 7; [2011] 2 F.L.R. 1. The use of the "balance sheet" approach in determining the best interests of an incapacitated adult was considered in *Re M (Adult Patient) (Minimally Conscious State: Withdrawal of Treatment)* [2011] EWHC 2443 (Fam); [2012] 1 W.L.R. 1653. Baker J found that it was appropriate in the case of a patient in a minimally conscious (rather than vegetative) state who is clinically stable ([245]). However, the application to withdraw artificial nutrition and hydration was dismissed as, in this case, the importance of preserving life was the decisive factor ([249]). The case has been frequently referred to cited since, including *St George's Healthcare NHS Trust v P* [2015] EWCOP 42; [2015] Med. L.R. 463. See also *An NHS Foundation Trust v M and K* [2013] EWHC 2402 (COP). Eleanor King J stated that whilst the presumption in favour of preservation of life is a fundamental principle, "it does not displace the patient's best interests as the paramount consideration for the Court" [59]. Further, a central (but not the only) question is whether treatment would be "futile or overly burdensome" or whether it is a case where there is no prospect of recovery [61].

[119] *Aintree University Hospitals NHS Foundation Trust v James* [2013] UKSC 67; [2014] A.C. 591 at [22]. Note here the ratio of Lady Hale in *Aintree* (with whom Lord Neuberger, Lord Clarke, Lord Carnwath and Lord Hughes agreed), which applies mutatis mutandis where the withdrawal of treatment concerns a child: see decision of Lord Justice Baker (with whom Laing LJ and King LJ agreed) in *Parfitt v Guy's and St Thomas' Children's NHS Foundation Trust* [2021] EWCA Civ 362 at [12], in which *Aintree* was followed. Note, further, the guidance in the Mental Capacity Act 2005 and the Code of Conduct (2007), in particular as to when "treatment is futile, overly burdensome to the patient or where there is no prospect of recovery" at 5.31.

[120] [2013] UKSC 67; [2014] A.C. 591 at [39].

Children

Replace paragraph 13-050 (to incorporate updates to footnotes 123 and 124) with:

13-050   If a child has capacity to consent to medical treatment, the same principles apply as to an adult. There is a statutory presumption that a child has the same capacity to consent to treatment as an adult from the age of 16.[121] A child under 16 is capable of consenting to medical treatment, provided he is "*Gillick* competent", i.e. provided he or she has sufficient maturity to understand the implications of the proposed treatment[122] and the consequences of refusal of treatment.[123] However, where a child who is "*Gillick* competent" declines to consent to treatment, his parents or the court can do so on his behalf.[124] Further, in the exercise of its wardship jurisdiction, the court may override a parent's wishes for treatment of a child.[125] However, the court will not order that a particular medical procedure be administered where consent to treatment is not forthcoming from the child or from those with power to consent on his behalf. The decision as to the appropriate treatment in the best interests of the patient is then for his attending doctors and not for the court.[126]

[121] Family Law Reform Act 1969 s.8(1). The presumption may be rebutted.

[122] See *Gillick v West Norfolk and Wisbech AHA* [1986] A.C. 112.

[123] See, e.g. *Re E (A Minor) (Wardship: Medical Treatment)* [1993] 1 F.L.R. 386 FamD: a 15-year-old Jehovah's Witness was not competent to refuse a blood transfusion because although he understood that he would die, he did not realise the full implications of the process of dying: transfusion lawful. In relation to para.13-050 generally, see too *AB v CD, Tavistock and Portman NHS Foundation Trust* [2021] EWHC 741 (Fam); [2021] Med. L.R. 365 (Lieven J) and *Bell v Tavistock and Portman NHS Trust* [2021] EWCA Civ 1363; [2022] 1 All E.R. 416 (Lord Burnett, Sir Geoffrey Vos, King LJ).

[124] See *Re W (A Minor) (Medical Treatment: The Court's Jurisdiction)* [1993] Fam. 64 CA (authorisation of removal to special hospital and treatment of 16-year-old anorexic), more recently considered and applied in *X (A Child) (No.2) A NHS Trust v X* [2021] EWHC 65 (Fam); [2021] 4 W.L.R. 11 (Sir James Munby).

[125] See, e.g. *Re O (A Minor) (Medical Treatment)* [1993] 4 Med. L.R. 272, where Johnson J overrode parents' refusal of a blood transfusion in the event that the child's condition deteriorated to the point at which the transfusion was necessary. By contrast, see *Re T (A Minor) Wardship: Medical Treatment* [1997] 1 W.L.R. 242 CA, where parents' refusal to consent to a liver transplant operation was upheld.

[126] See *Portsmouth NHS Trust v Wyatt* [2004] EWHC 2247 (Fam); [2005] 1 F.L.R. 21 and on appeal [2005] EWCA Civ 1181; [2005] 1 W.L.R. 3995. As to the question of the child's "best interests", the Court of Appeal rejected the test (applied at first instance) of whether life would be "intolerable" for the child.

(g)   Hospitals and Health Authorities

Vicarious liability

Replace footnote 128 with:

[128] For a discussion of vicarious liability, which is beyond the scope of this book, see *Clerk & Lindsell on Torts* (2020, 2nd supp, 2022), Ch.6. See too, Jones, *Medical Negligence* (2021) Chs 9 and 11 (as relevant). **13-052**

4.   DAMAGES

(b)   Factual Causation

Warnings

Replace footnote 218 with:

[218] See *Diamond v Royal Devon & Exeter NHS Foundation Trust* [2019] EWCA Civ 585; [2019] Med. L.R. 273. See also *Watts v North Bristol NHS Trust* [2022] EWHC 2048 (QB) where the judge held that a claimant was not told properly of alternative procedures but the claimant failed to establish that, if told, he would have elected such an alternative. Note, however, that where a claimant sues in trespass, on the grounds that he was not told even in broad terms the nature of the treatment proposed, he need not prove that he would have acted in any way differently: *Chatterton v Gerson* [1981] Q.B. 432 QB at 442H–443A. **13-090**

(e)   Measure of Damages

(i)   Damages for Personal Injury

Replace footnote 241 with:

[241] Quantum of damages for personal injuries is too vast a topic for this book and is more than adequately dealt with elsewhere, e.g. W. Norris and others (eds), *Kemp & Kemp: The Quantum of Damages in Personal Injury and Fatal Accident Claims*, Rel.164 (London: Sweet & Maxwell, 2022). This chapter highlights some important issues relating to the quantum of damages in the context of clinical negligence. **13-105**

(iii)   Damages in Wrongful Birth and Wrongful Conception Claims

Unwanted healthy child born to a disabled mother

Replace footnote 254 with:

[254] The sum awarded was £15,000. In *Less v Hussain* [2012] EWHC 3513 (QB); [2013] Med. L.R. 383 Judge Cotter QC declined (albeit obiter) to extend the availability of a "*Rees* award" to a "wrongful conception" case where the baby was stillborn. Note also that *Rees* was relied upon by the claimant **13-111**

children in *A v A Health and Social Services Trust* [2011] NICA 28; [2012] N.I. 77, who sought damages to compensate them for the fact that, due to an error on the part of the defendant health authority in carrying out an in vitro fertilisation (IVF) procedure, which led to the sperm used in the process coming from a donor with a different ethnicity from that of the claimants' mother and non-biological father, the claimants had inherited a different skin colour than their parents. The Court of Appeal in Northern Ireland rejected the claim, holding that "having a different skin colour from the majority of the surrounding population and their parents [could not] sensibly be regarded as damage or disability". See too, *ARB v IVF Hammersmith* [2018] EWCA Civ 2803 (Davies LJ).

(v) Recovery of Damages Prevented by Doctrine of Illegality

Replace footnote 261 with:

13-117   ²⁶¹ [2020] UKSC 43; [2021] A.C. 563. See the Medical Law Reports for several recent applications of this decision.

CHAPTER 14

REGULATION OF FINANCIAL SERVICES

1. GENERAL

Replace paragraph 14-001 (to incorporate updates to footnotes) with:

This chapter provides an overview of the regulatory regime under the Financial **14-001**
Services and Markets Act 2000 (FSMA), as amended, to the extent relevant to this work. Some changes to the regime were made by the Banking Act 2009, the Financial Services Act 2010 and the Financial Services (Banking Reform) Act 2013 in the wake of the global financial crisis of the late 2000s. Further substantial amendments to FSMA were made by the Financial Services Act 2012,[1] implementing the new ("twin peaks") regulatory architecture devised by the then Coalition government. Aspects of the FSMA regime apply to a large number of businesses in the financial services sector of the economy, ranging from large banks and insurers to one-man financial advisers. Accordingly, it is convenient to deal with them in a discrete chapter. It is, however, beyond the scope of this chapter to provide a detailed review of the law relating to regulation of financial services in the UK. FSMA and related material, including other legislation, subsidiary legislation, rules, codes, European directives and published guidance, are extensive, complex and frequently change. Reference should be made to specialist works.[2] It is also beyond the scope of this chapter to deal with the law relating to banking, insurance and pensions. The main focus is upon those activities of financial practitioners, principally those relating to investment, which are within the scope of the FSMA regulatory regime.

[1] See *A new approach to financial regulation: the blueprint for reform* (HMT, June 2011). Most of the Financial Services Act 2012 came into force on 1 April 2013. Note also the amendments made by the Bank of England and Financial Services Act 2016 and the Financial Services Act 2021; and the future (extensive) amendments to FSMA envisaged under the Financial Services and Markets Bill 2022-23.

[2] For the text on such material and detailed commentary, see J. Kirk, R. Kingham and others (eds), *Encyclopedia of Financial Services Law*, Rel.130 (London: Sweet & Maxwell, 2022).

(a) The Regulators

Replace paragraph 14-004 (to incorporate updates to footnotes 11 and 13) with:

FSMA originally conferred all regulatory powers on a single statutory regula- **14-004**
tor, the Financial Services Authority (FSA), with the Treasury retaining overall responsibility for the regulatory regime as a whole. The regulatory capacity of the FSA was remarkably large in terms of scope, powers and discretion. It regulated the whole of the financial sector and concerned itself with both prudential and conduct of business aspects. The FSA had very wide-ranging powers of rule-making,[5] authorisation of firms,[6] approval of key personnel,[7] monitoring, investigation, intervention and discipline.[8] It also undertook the official listing function as the competent authority under EC Directives, styling itself as "UKLA" (the UK Listing Authority).[9] Since the reform of the regulatory architecture effected by the Financial Services Act 2012,[10] the "micro" prudential regulation of bank and other

systemically important financial institutions (SIFIs) as well as all insurers is now undertaken by the PRA,[11] acting through the Prudential Regulation Committee (PRC) of the Bank of England,[12] and the FSA has been replaced by the FCA[13] with the narrower remit of regulating conduct of business and markets (and prudentially regulating non-SIFIs). The PRA and FCA have the same wide powers as the FSA, as is consistent with their respective remits, and there are complex provisions as to the division of those powers and as to liaison between the two regulators. The PRA regulatory regime and those aspects of the FCA regulatory regime as applying only to "PRA-authorised persons"[14] are beyond the scope of this chapter.

[5] See FSMA Pt X, "Rules and Guidance". The FSA also had power to make rules under many other provisions in the Act. To reflect the amendment of FSMA by the Financial Services Act 2012 to make provision for the new regulatory architecture (see below), Pt X has been replaced by Pt 9A (ss.137A–141A).

[6] See FSMA Pt IV (ss.40–55, "Permission to carry on Regulated Activities"). See further para.14-013. To reflect the amendment of FSMA by the Financial Services Act 2012 to make provision for the new regulatory architecture (see below), Pt IV has been replaced by Pt 4A (ss.55A–55Z4).

[7] See FSMA ss.59–70. See further paras 14-015 and 14-016.

[8] The broad nature of FSA's powers is apparent from the titles to the following Parts of FSMA that conferred various powers upon it (and now the FCA and PRA): Pt V (ss.56–71,"Performance of Regulated Activities"); Pt VII (ss.104–117,"Control of Business Transfers"); Pt VIII (ss.118–131,"Provisions relating to Market Abuse"); Pt VIIIA (131B–131K, added by the Financial Services Act 2010, "Short selling"); Pt XI (ss.165–177, "Information Gathering and Investigations"); Pt XII (ss.178–192, "Control over Authorised Persons"); Pt 12A (ss.192A–192N, "Powers exercisable in relation to parent undertakings"), Pt XIII (ss.193–204, "Incoming Firms: Intervention by Authority"); Pt XIV (ss.205–211,"Disciplinary Measures"); Pt XVII (ss.235–284,"Collective Investment Schemes"); Pt XVIII, ss.285–301, "Recognised Investment Exchanges and Clearing Houses"); Pt 18A (ss.313A–313D, Suspension and removal of financial instruments from trading); Pt XIX, ss.314–324, "Lloyd's"); Pt XX (ss.325–333, ("Provision of Financial Services by Members of the Professions"); Pt XXI (ss.334–339, "Mutual Societies"); Pt XXII (ss.340–346) ("Auditors and Actuaries"); Pt XXIII (ss.347–354, "Public Record, Disclosure of Information and Co-operation"); Pt XXIV (ss.355–379, "Insolvency"); Pt XXV (ss.380–386, "Injunctions and Restitution"); and Pt XXVI (ss.387–396, "Notices").

[9] FSMA Pt VI ss.72–103. The FSA took over as the "competent authority" from the (London) Stock Exchange after it demutualised in May 2000. The FCA (see below) has taken over this function and FSMA Pt VI has been amended by the Financial Services Act 2012 accordingly.

[10] In force on 1 April 2013. See FSMA Pt 1A (the new regulators), Sch.1ZA (FCA) and Sch.1ZB (PRA), as inserted by the Financial Services Act 2012.

[11] The PRA's website is http://www.bankofengland.co.uk/pra/Pages/default.aspx [Accessed 23 September 2022].

[12] Originally the PRA was a subsidiary of the Bank but the change of status was given effect by the Bank of England and Financial Services Act 2016: see FSMA new s.2A and the new Pt 3A of the Bank of England Act 1998, added by the 2016 Act, ss.12 and 13, respectively.

[13] The FCA's website is https://www.fca.org.uk [Accessed 23 September 2022].

[14] As defined in FSMA s.2B(5).

Replace paragraph 14-005 (to incorporate updates to footnotes 16 and 17) with:

14-005   The Act requires the regulators to discharge their "general functions" within a framework of defined "regulatory objectives" and having regard to eight regulatory principles, although these operate at a very general level and are not expressed to be applicable to specific decisions.[15] The Act provides for a compensation scheme[16] and an ombudsman scheme (the Financial Ombudsman Service or FOS).[17] Some decisions of the regulators, primarily their disciplinary decisions, are subject to appeal to the Upper Tribunal.[18] The regulators remain subject to judicial review in the exercise of their functions under FSMA, as under the 1986 Act.[19]

[15] For the "objectives" of the FCA and PRA: see FSMA ss.1B–1K (FCA) and ss.2B–2J (PRA), as inserted by the Financial Services Act 2012 and amended by the Financial Services (Banking Reform) Act 2013 ss.1 and 2. For the principles, see FSMA s.3B.

[16] FSMA Pt XV ss.212–224A. See paras 14-143 to 14-158.

[17] FSMA Pt XVI ss.225–234B. See paras 14-121 to 14-141.

[18] Established under the Tribunals, Courts and Enforcement Act 2007. FSMA Pt IX originally established a Financial Services and Markets Tribunal (FISMAT) but its functions were transferred to the Upper Tribunal by SI 2010/22. There is an appeal on a point of law to the Court of Appeal (TCEA 2007 s.13). See *Financial Services Authority v Fox Hayes* [2009] EWCA Civ 76; [2009] 1 B.C.L.C. 603 (successful appeal by the FSA from FISMAT on whether approvals of advertisements by authorised persons contravened the *FSA Handbook* (COBS Module), see paras 14-059 onwards). See also *Winterflood Securities Ltd v Financial Services Authority* [2010] EWCA Civ 423; [2010] 1 B.C.L.C. 502 (an unsuccessful appeal by the appellant in relation to an FSA market abuse determination) and *Burns v Financial Conduct Authority* [2017] EWCA Civ 2140; [2018] 1 W.L.R. 4161 (unsuccessful appeal by approved person). See also *Jeffery v Financial Services Authority* [2012] EWCA Civ 178 (successful appeal from Tribunal decision on point of law relating to time limit under FSMA s.66(5)(a)); *Financial Conduct Authority v Hobbs* [2013] EWCA Civ 918; [2013] Bus L.R. 1290 (FCA traders successful appeal against Tribunal decision); *7722656 Canada Inc (formerly Swift Trade Inc) v Financial Services Authority* [2013] EWCA Civ 1662; [2014] Lloyd's Rep. F.C. 207 (appeal against FSA in market abuse context dismissed); *Abdul Razzaq v Financial Services Authority* [2014] EWCA Civ 770 (applicant refused permission to appeal Tribunal decision); *Financial Conduct Authority v Macris* [2017] UKSC 19; [2017] 1 W.L.R. 1095 (on FSMA 2000 s.393: Tribunal ruling against FCA reversed). And see *Bayliss & Co (Financial Services) Ltd, Clive John Rosier v Financial Conduct Authority* [2015] UKUT 265 (TCC) (the Tribunal issued recommendations to the FCA regarding its procedures in relation to the publication of decision notices that had been referred to the tribunal).

[19] As was the case in relation to the FSA (and its predecessor, the SIB). For examples of (unsuccessful) applications against the SIB, see *R. v Securities and Investments Board Ex p. Independent Financial Advisers Association* [1995] 2 B.C.L.C. 76; *R. v Securities and Investments Board Ex p. Sun Life Assurance Society Plc* [1996] 2 B.C.L.C. 150. For (unsuccessful) judicial reviews of the FSA, see (i) *R. v Financial Services Authority Ex p. Davies* [2003] EWCA Civ 1128; [2004] 1 W.L.R. 185; (ii) *R. (on the application of Griggs) v Financial Services Authority* [2008] EWHC 2587 (Admin); [2009] A.C.D. 28 (FSA's decision to depart from the procedure set out in the "EG" ("Enforcement Guidance") part of the Handbook (a procedure that was explicitly stated not to be applicable in all cases)); (iii) *R. (on the application of Amro International SA) v Financial Services Authority* [2010] EWCA Civ 123; [2010] 3 All E.R. 723 (FSA's decision to require the disclosure of certain documents at the request of the US regulator, the SEC); (iv) *R. (on the application of the British Bankers Association) v Financial Services Authority* [2011] EWHC 999 (Admin); [2011] Bus. L.R. 1531 (FSA's PPI complaints scheme); (v) *R. (on the application of S) v Financial Services Authority* [2011] EWHC 1645 (Admin) (FSA's decision to publish decision notice); (vi) *R. (on the application of C) v Financial Services Authority* [2013] EWCA Civ 677 (*R. v Financial Services Authority Ex p. Davies* [2003] EWCA Civ 1128 followed); (vii) *R. (on the application of Julien Grout) v Financial Conduct Authority* [2015] EWHC 596 (Admin).

(b)   The General Prohibition

Territorial scope

Replace paragraph 14-009 (to incorporate deletion of text and update to footnote 42) with:

The general prohibition relates only to the carrying on of a regulated activity *in the UK*. The wording is apt to cover "inward" activity that affects the UK market.[41] As regards "outward" activity by persons in the UK targeting an overseas market, further provision is made in FSMA.[42]   **14-009**

[41] In *Financial Services Authority v Bayshore Nominees Ltd* [2009] EWHC 285 (Ch); [2009] Lloyd's Rep. F.C. 398, it was confirmed that "inward" advice from persons outside the UK, targeting UK investors, was carried on "in the United Kingdom". See also *Financial Conduct Authority v Capital Alternatives Ltd* unreported 26 March 2018 ChD ([2018] 3 WLUK 623) (location of establishment and operation of collective investment scheme). But note that there are significant exclusions in the RAO (as to

which see para.14-028) for investment business activity by "overseas persons" (defined in RAO art.3), e.g. RAO art.72(1)(2).

[42] FSMA s.418, as amended.

(d) Authorised Persons

In paragraph 14-012, replace "Part IVA" with:

14-012 Part 4A

14-013 *Change title of paragraph:*

Part 4A permission

Replace paragraph 14-013 (to incorporate updates to text and footnotes) with:
Part 4A of FSMA[61] contains elaborate provisions relating to the grant of "Part 4A permission" to domestic concerns to carry on regulated activities. The regulators are given a very wide discretion, especially in relation to the scope and terms of any permission they grant.[62] They may impose limitations[63] and requirements[64] as to how a person is, or is not, to act. Importantly, the regulators must ensure that the person concerned will satisfy and will continue to satisfy the "threshold conditions" in Sch.6 in relation to a regulated activity.[65] Of central importance are the requirements that the person concerned has adequate resources and is suitable (i.e. fit and proper).

[61] ss.55A–55Z4. The Financial Services Act 2021 amended Pt 4A of FSMA by inserting s.55JA and a new Sch.6A to provide an additional process for the FCA to vary or cancel Pt 4A permissions. These amendments entered into force on 1 July 2021.

[62] FSMA ss55E–55G.

[63] FSMA ss.55E(5), 55F(4).

[64] FSMA ss.55L–55PB. This may include an "assets requirement" (s.55P(4)) entailing the freezing of assets or their transfer to a trustee.

[65] FSMA s.55B and Sch.6, as amended. See also the "COND" Module of the *FCA Handbook* (para.14-042).

The "sandbox"

Replace footnote 66 with:

14-014 [66] See its website *https://www.fca.org.uk/firms/regulatory-sandbox* [Accessed 23 September 2022].

(e) Approved Persons, etc

Replace footnote 67 with:

14-015 [67] FSMA ss.59–71I.

Replace paragraph 14-016 (to incorporate updates to text and footnote 70) with:

14-016 The Bank of England and Financial Services Act 2016 (Commencement No.6 and Transitional Provisions) Regulations 2019 (SI 2019/1136), published on 18 July 2019, extend the SM&CR to insurers with effect from 10 December 2018, and provide for a further extension of the SM&CR to FCA solo-regulated firms (except for benchmark administrators), from 9 December 2019. As a consequence the SM&CR has replaced the approved persons regime for most firms.[70]

[70] See the Bank of England and Financial Services Act 2016 (Commencement No.6 and Transitional Provisions) Regulations 2019 (SI 2019/1136). In July 2021, the Treasury published a Consultation Paper,

Senior Managers & Certification Regime: Financial Market Infrastructures proposing an SM&CR for financial market infrastructures; and in the FCA's 2022 Perimeter Report, published in July 2022, the FCA referred to extending the SM&CR to recognised investment exchanges, credit rating agencies, payments and e-money firms.

(f) Exempt Persons

Replace paragraph 14-017 (to incorporate updates to text and footnote 72) with:

FSMA makes provision for certain "exempt persons".[71] Three categories of **14-017** person are exempt: (1) "appointed representatives" of authorised persons and certain tied agents operating outside of the UK[72]; (2) recognised investment exchanges and recognised clearing houses[73]; and (3) persons specified, or within a class specified, by Treasury order.[74] Exempt persons do not contravene the general prohibition if they carry on a regulated activity in the UK as long as they are exempt persons *in relation to that activity*. Unlike authorised person status, exempt person status is generally conferred to a limited extent in relation to certain regulated activities. Thus if exempt persons stray outside such activities, they lose exempt person status and breach the general prohibition (unless they become authorised in respect of that other activity). Although exempt persons are subject to the financial promotion restriction,[75] the relevant Treasury order exempts non-real-time and solicited real-time communications made or directed by an exempt person for the purposes of his business in relation to which he is exempt.[76]

[71] Defined in FSMA s.417(1).

[72] FSMA ss.39–39A. See further paras 14-018 to 14-020.

[73] FSMA s.285.

[74] FSMA s.38. See the FSMA (Exemption) Order 2002 (SI 2001/1201) as extensively amended.

[75] See para.14-010.

[76] The FPO art.16. See para.14-031. And see art.15(1)(b): financial promotion restriction does not apply to certain "real time" [introductions to] exempt persons.

(g) Appointed Representatives

Replace paragraph 14-018 (to incorporate updates to text and footnotes 77 and 78) with:

Persons authorised to carry on regulated activities under FSMA, including **14-018** product provider firms and independent intermediaries, frequently do so through agents called "appointed representatives".[77] Specific provision is made for them under FSMA.[78] An appointed representative, rather than being required to become an authorised person, is accorded exempt person status,[79] but only so long as an authorised person, termed his "principal", takes responsibility (including regulatory responsibility) for him. Thus regulation of appointed representatives is, to some extent, sub-contracted to authorised persons.[80] The principal authorised person's Pt 4A permission must extend to all of his appointed representatives' activities. A person cannot simultaneously be both an appointed representative in respect of some activities and an authorised person in relation to others.[81]

[77] FSMA ss.417(1) and 39(2). And see s.39A ("tied agents" acting outside UK).

[78] FSMA s.39, as amended to make special provision for principals who are credit institutions or mortgage intermediaries: see new s.39(1ZA). See also FSMA s.39A in respect of certain tied agents operating outside of the UK.

[79] See para.14-017.

80 See especially FSMA s.39(3) and (4).

81 FSMA s.39(1) (the words in parenthesis).

(h) Members of Professions

Replace footnote 107 with:

14-022 107 i.e. by obtaining "Part 4A permission": see para.14-013.

(i) European Aspects

Replace paragraph 14-024 (to incorporate update to text) with:

14-024 The future of such EU-derived law in the UK in the wake of the "Brexit" referendum remains a live issue at the time of writing, despite the deal reached in December 2020 (as per the UK-EU Trade and Co-operation Agreement and associated declarations) and the end of the Brexit transition period. The Financial Services Act 2021 has recently made, and will in the future make, extensive amendments to the legislative and regulatory framework for financial services arising from the UK's departure from the EU, including to FSMA itself. Further significant reforms, including to FSMA itself, are envisaged under the Financial Services and Markets Bill 2022-23. The Government also made a number of statutory instruments, under the European Union (Withdrawal) Act 2018, to reflect the UK's status as a third country outside of the EU: see for example the Financial Services and Markets Act 2000 (Amendment) (EU Exit) Regulations 2019 (SI 2019/632), the EEA Passport Rights (Amendment, etc., and Transitional Provisions) (EU Exit) Regulations 2018 (SI 2018/1149) and the Collective Investment Schemes (Amendment etc.) (EU Exit) Regulations (SI 2019/325). It seems very likely, if not inevitable, that the approaches taken to regulating financial services in the EU and the UK respectively will diverge in the future.

2. APPLICATION OF THE FSMA REGULATORY REGIME

(a) Regulated Activities

The RAO

Replace paragraph 14-029 (to incorporate updates to footnotes) with:

14-029 The scheme of Pt II of the RAO[143] is, broadly, to incorporate under "chapters" a series of articles relating to a "specified activity." The first article in the chapter defines the substantive activity and other articles define specific exclusions or contain supplemental provisions. In addition, there are some general exclusions that apply to several specified kinds of activity.[144] Regulated activities that are specified activities relating to an "investment" (also as specified in the RAO)[145] comprise the following: (1) accepting deposits[146]; (2) issuing electronic money[147]; (3) effecting and carrying out contracts of insurance[148]; (4) dealing in investments as principal[149]; (5) dealing in investments as agent[150]; (6) bidding in emissions auctions[151]; (7) arranging deals in investments[152]; (8) credit broking[153]; (9) operating an electronic system in relation to lending (i.e. so-called "P2P lending")[154]; (10) managing investments[155]; (11) assisting in the administration and performance of a contract of insurance[156]; (12) activities in relation to debt[157]; (13) safeguarding and administering investments[158]; (14) sending dematerialised instructions[159]; (15) establishing, etc. a collective investment scheme[160]; (16) establishing, etc. a pension scheme[161]; (17) providing basic advice on stakeholder products[162]; (18) advising on investments[163]; (19) advising, managing and arranging activities in relation to Lloyd's[164]; (20) entering as provider into a funeral plan contract[165]; (21) activities in relation to regulated credit agreements[166]; (22) activities in relation to regulated hire agreements[167]; (23) entering into a regulated mortgage contract or administering the same[168]; (24) entering into a regulated home reversion plan (HRP) or administering the same[169]; (25) entering into a regulated home purchase plan (HPP) or administering the same[170]; (26) entering into a regulated sale and rent back agreement (SRA) or administering the same[171]; (27) activities of reclaim funds in meeting repayment claims and managing dormant account money[172]; (28) activities in relation to specified benchmarks[173]; and (29) agreeing to carry on certain specified activities.[174] Each of such activities is defined in considerable detail in the RAO and it is essential to have regard to the definitions including any applicable exclusions.[175]

[143] RAO Pt II arts 4–72J.

[144] RAO Pt II arts 66–72J.

[145] RAO Pt III arts 73–89.

[146] i.e. banking. RAO Pt II Ch.II art.5; it is subject to the exclusions in arts 5–9AC.

[147] RAO Ch.IIA art.9B; it is subject to the exclusions in arts 9C–9G (but see art.9BA); see also supplemental provisions in arts 9H–9L. This chapter was extensively amended on the implementation of the Second E-Money Directive 2009/110, by SI 2011/99 (and see PERG3A of the *FCA Handbook*).

[148] RAO Ch.III art.10; it is subject to the exclusions in arts 11–12B; see also provision in art.13 in relation to Lloyds.

[149] RAO Ch.IV art.14; it is subject to the exclusions in arts 15–20, 66, 68–72AA and 72H.

[150] RAO Ch.V art.21; it is subject to the exclusions in arts 22–24, 67–72B, 72D, 72G and 72H.

[151] RAO Ch.VA arts 24A–24B.

[152] RAO Ch.VI arts 25–25E. The exclusions (see arts 26–36, 66–72D, 72G and 72H) vary, depending on the category of "arrangements" and investments involved. See *Re Inertia Partnership LLP* [2007] EWHC 539 (Ch); [2007] 1 B.C.L.C. 739 on the meaning of "arrangements" in the RAO art.25, followed in *Watersheds Ltd v DaCosta* [2009] EWHC 1299 (QB); [2009] 2 B.C.L.C. 515. But note that the FSA "clarified" the effect of *DaCosta* in its Handbook (now the *FCA Handbook*), PERG 2.7.2B adding that the judgment "should be considered in the light of the case to which it relates". See also, *Personal Touch Financial Services Ltd v SimplySure Ltd* [2016] EWCA Civ 461; [2016] Bus. L.R. 1049, followed in *Financial Conduct Authority v Capital Alternatives Ltd* unreported 26 March 2018 ChD ([2018] 3 WLUK 623) and *Financial Conduct Authority v Avacade Ltd (In Liquidation)* [2021] EWCA Civ 1206.

[153] RAO Ch VIA arts 36A–36G.

[154] RAO Ch VIB, arts 36H–36J.

[155] RAO Ch.VII art.37; it is subject to the exclusions in arts 38 and 39, 66, 68, 69, 72C and 72E.

[156] RAO Ch.VIIA arts 39A and 39B; it is subject to the exclusions in arts 39C, 66, 67, 72AA–72D, 72G and 72H.

[157] RAO Ch.VIIB arts.39D–39M.

[158] RAO Ch.VIII art.40; it is subject to the exclusions in arts 41–44, 66–69, 71, 72AA, 72C and 72H.

[159] RAO Ch.IX art.45; it is subject to the exclusions in arts 46–50, 66, 69, 72AA and 72H.

[160] RAO Ch.X arts 51ZA–51ZE; it is subject to the exclusions in arts 51A and 51ZF to 51ZG. Note the extensive amendments to Ch.X as a result of the implementation of the AIFMD (Alternative Investment Fund Managers Directive 2011/61) by the Alternative Investment Fund Managers Regulations 2013 (SI 2013/1773).

[161] RAO Ch.XI art.52, as amended; it is subject to the exclusions in art.52A.

[162] RAO Ch.XIA art.52B, added by SI 2004/2737 and replaced by SI 2005/593. It is subject to the exclusions in s.52C.

[163] RAO Ch.XII arts 53–53E, as amended by SI 2017/488 (transposing the MiFID II definition of a "personal recommendation"). The exclusions (see arts 54–55, 66–70, 72–72B, 72D, 72G and 72H) vary depending on the category of investments involved. For case law discussing the meaning of "investment advice", see: *Re Market Wizard Systems (UK) Ltd* [1998] 2 B.C.L.C. 282; *Martin v Britannia Life Ltd* [2000] Lloyd's Rep. P.N. 412 (considered further at paras 15-027 and 15-059); *Walker v Inter-Alliance Group Plc (In Administration), Scottish Equitable Plc* [2007] EWHC 1858 (Ch); [2007] Pens. L.R. 347, considered further at para.15-088; *Financial Services Authority v Bayshore Nominees Ltd* [2009] EWHC 285 (Ch); [2009] Lloyd's Rep. F.C. 398.

[164] RAO Ch.XIII arts 56–58; it is subject to the exclusion in art.58A.

[165] RAO Ch.XIV art.59; it is subject to the exclusions in arts 60, 60ZA and 60AA.

[166] RAO Ch.XIVA arts 60B–60M.

[167] RAO Ch.XIVB arts 60N–60S.

[168] RAO Ch.XV art.61; it is subject to the exclusions in arts 62–63A, 66, 72–72AA, 72G and 72I. This chapter was extensively amended as a result of the Mortgage Credit Directive (Directive 2014/17).

[169] RAO Ch.XVA art.63B, added by SI 2006/2383. Art.63B(2) is subject to the exclusions in arts 63C–63D. The whole of art.63B is subject to the exclusions in arts 66, 72, 72AA and 72G.

[170] RAO Ch.XVB art.63F, added by SI 2006/2383. Art.63F(2) is subject to the exclusions in arts 63G–63I. The whole of art.63F is subject to the exclusions in, arts 66, 72, 72AA and 72G.

[171] RAO Ch.XVC art.63J, added by SI 2009/1342. Article 63J(2) is subject to the exclusions in arts 63–63L. The whole of art.63J is subject to the exclusions in, arts 66, 72, 72AA and 72G.

[172] RAO Ch.XVD art.63N, added by SI 2009/1389. There are no exclusions.

[173] RAO Ch.XVE arts 63O–63T.

[174] RAO Ch.XVI art.64; it is subject to the exclusions in arts 5, 9B, 10, 25D, 25DA, 51ZA–51ZE, 52, 63N, 63S, 72, 72G and 72H.

[175] See the FCA's "Perimeter Guidance" (the PERG part of its Regulatory Guides at the end of its Handbook: see para.14-050).

(c) Investment

Replace footnote 217 with:

14-033 [217] FSMA s.235(1). *See Russell-Cooke Trust Co v Elliott* unreported 16 July 2001 ([2001] 7 WLUK 359), on the identically worded 1986 Act s.75; applied by Lindsay J in *Russell-Cooke Trust Co v Prentis (No. 1)* [2002] EWHC 2227 (Ch) (the "property" was mortgages); and *Financial Services Authority v Fradley* [2005] EWCA Civ 1183; [2006] 2 B.C.L.C. 616 (the "property" was bets placed on horse races). See also the "land banking" cases where the property was land: *Financial Services Authority v Watkins (t/a Consolidated Land UK)* [2011] EWHC 1976 (Ch); *Financial Conduct Authority v Capital Alternatives Ltd* [2014] EWHC 144 (Ch); [2014] 3 All E.R. 780; *Financial Services Authority v Asset LI Inc* [2016] UKSC 17; [2016] 3 All E.R. 93. A pooled fund to pay guaranteed rental income was arguably a CIS though the conveyancing solicitors involved were not engaged in the regulated activity of operating it (*Various Angelgate and Baltic House Claimants v Key Manchester Ltd* [2020] EWHC 3643 (Ch); [2021] P.N.L.R. 15).

4. REGULATORY RULES AND THE FCA HANDBOOK AND PRA RULEBOOK

(a) General

Replace footnote 237 with:

14-038 [237] See *http://www.prarulebook.co.uk/* [Accessed 23 September 2022].

Replace footnote 240 with:

[240] The FCA website is *https://www.fca.org.uk* [Accessed 23 September 2022] and the PRA's website is *http://www.bankofengland.co.uk/pra/Pages/default.aspx* [Accessed 23 September 2022].

(b) FCA Handbook

Replace footnote 241 with:

[241] See *https://www.handbook.fca.org.uk* [Accessed 23 September 2022].

14-039

To the end of the second paragraph, add:
   The FCA Handbook has also recently been updated to show the applicable rules following the end of the Brexit transition period.

(i) Structure of FCA Handbook

The Prudential Standards block

In paragraph 14-043, after "This contains", replace "eight" with:
   seven

14-043

Replace table with:

Reference Code	Title
GENPRU	*General Prudential sourcebook*
INSPRU	*Prudential sourcebook for Insurers*
MIFIDPRU	*Prudential sourcebook for MiFID Investment Firms*
MIPRU	*Prudential sourcebook for Mortgage and Home Finance Firms, and Insurance Intermediaries*
IPRU-FSOC	*Interim Prudential sourcebook for Friendly Societies*
IPRU-INS	*Interim Prudential sourcebook for Insurers*
IPRU-INV	*Interim Prudential sourcebook for Investment Businesses*

[245] Applies to most business sectors.

The Business Standards block

Replace table with:

14-044

Reference Code	Title	Subject matter[246]
COBS	*Conduct of Business Sourcebook*	Applies to all firms accepting deposits, conducting designated investment business and carrying on long-term business in relation to life policies
ICOBS	*Insurance: Conduct of Business sourcebook*	Applies to non-investment business of insurers
MCOB	*Mortgages and Home Finance: Conduct of Business sourcebook*	Applies to firms conducting regulated mortgage activities and home finances

Reference Code	Title	Subject matter[246]
BCOBS	*Banking: Conduct of Business sourcebook*	Applies to firms that accept deposits from banking customers
CMCOB	*Claims Management: Conduct of Business sourcebook*	Applies to claims management firms which were regulated by the FCA as of 1 April 2019
FPCOB	*Funeral Plan: Conduct of Business sourcebook*	Applies to firms that carry on regulated funeral plan activities and connected activities as of 29 July 2022
CASS	*Client Assets*	Rules and guidance on holding client assets and client moneys
MAR	*Market Conduct*	Applies to wholesale and professional markets
PROD	*Product Intervention and Product Governance Sourcebook*	Applies to MiFID investment firms, CRD credit institutions, MiFID optional exemption firms and branches of third country investment firms
ESG	*Environmental, Social and Governance sourcebook*	Rules and guidance concerning firms' approach to environmental, social and governance matters

[246] As described (where applicable) in the Reader's Guide.

Listing, Prospectus and Disclosure block

14-048   *Replace table with:*

Reference Code	Title
LR	*Listing Rules*
PRR	*Prospectus Regulation Rules sourcebook*
DTR	*Disclosure Guidance and Transparency Rules sourcebook*
DISC	*Product Disclosure sourcebook*

(v)   Treatment

In paragraph 14-056, after "ICOBS) and the", replace "Mortgage and Home Finance Conduce" with:

14-056   Mortgages and Home Finance Conduct

(c) Principles for Businesses

Replace table with: 14-057

1	*Integrity*	A firm must conduct its business with integrity.
2	*Skill, care and diligence*	A firm must conduct its business with due skill, care and diligence.
3	*Management and control*	A firm must take reasonable care to organise and control its affairs responsibly and effectively, with adequate risk management systems.
4	*Financial prudence*	A firm must maintain adequate financial resources.
5	*Market conduct*	A firm must observe proper standards of market conduct.
6	*Customers' interests*	A firm must pay due regard to the interests of its customers and treat them fairly.
7	*Communications with clients*	A firm must pay due regard to the information needs of its clients, and communicate information to them in a way which is clear, fair and not misleading.
8	*Conflicts of interest*	A firm must manage conflicts of interest fairly, both between itself and its customers and between a customer and another client.
9	*Customers: relationships of trust*	A firm must take reasonable care to ensure the suitability of its advice and discretionary decisions for any customer who is entitled to rely upon its judgment.
10	*Clients' assets*	A firm must arrange adequate protection for clients' assets when it is responsible for them.
11	*Relations with regulators*	A firm must deal with its regulators in an open and co-operative way, and must disclose to the FCA appropriately anything relating to the firm of which that regulator would reasonably expect notice.[267]

[267] As of 31 July 2023 the FCA intends to implement a 12th Principle, namely the Consumer Duty. There will be extensive, associated rule changes to support the creation of the Consumer Duty, which are described in detail in the FCA's Policy Statement PS22/9 (July 2022). The underlying purpose is to require firms dealing with consumers to take a consumer-centric approach to all aspects of their business, including product development, price and value setting, and information and support.

(e)   Conduct of Business Sourcebook (COBS)

(iii)   Conduct of Business Obligations

COBS 2.1: Acting honestly, fairly and professionally

Replace footnote 290 with:

14-063   290 See COBS 2.1.1. In *CMC Spreadbet Plc v Tchenguiz* [2022] EWHC 1640 (Comm) it was held that a spread betting firm's duty under COBS 2.1.1R to act in its client's best interest did not apply to its decision to close out the client's positions following a margin call.

(iv)   Categorisation of Clients

Replace footnote 303 with:

14-068   303 Defined in the Glossary and see COBS 3.5. On the interpretation of COBS 3.5.9R, see *Bank Leumi (UK) Plc v Wachner* [2011] EWHC 656 (Comm); [2011] 1 C.L.C. 454. For an example of an unsuccessful argument that a client had been wrongly categorised as a professional client, rather than a retail client, on the basis that he had not been given warnings as required by COBS, see *CMC Spreadbet Plc v Tchenguiz* [2022] EWHC 1640 (Comm).

(v)   Communicating with Clients

Replace paragraph 14-070 (to incorporate updates to text) with:

14-070   COBS 5 imposes specific disclosure obligations on firms that carry on any distance marketing activity from an establishment in the UK, with or for a consumer[315] in the UK. Generally,[316] a firm is required to provide a consumer with the requisite distance marketing information in good time before the consumer is bound by a distance contract or offer.[317] The information must be provided in a clear and comprehensible manner in any way appropriate to the means of distance communication used, with due regard, in particular, to the principles of good faith in commercial transactions, and the legal principles governing the protection of those who are unable to give their consent, such as minors.[318] These rules are mandatory and cannot be waived by the consumer.[319] Moreover, if a firm proposes to enter into a distance contract with a consumer that will be governed by the law of a country outside the UK, the firm must ensure that the consumer will not lose the protection created by the rules in COBS 5 if the distance contract has a close link with the territory of the UK.[320]

315 Generally, any natural person acting for purposes outside his trade, business or profession. Note that obligations relating to retail clients and to clients in MiFID or equivalent third country business falling outside the definition of "consumer" are dealt with under separate rules in COBS (see, e.g. COBS 8).

316 Note that a more limited obligation is imposed for certain contracts for payment services to which the Payment Services Regulations apply: see COBS 5.1.13A. There are also a number of exceptions: see COBS 5.1.7 onwards.

317 COBS 5.1.1. And see COBS 5.1.5–5.1.6 (terms and conditions, and form) and COBS 5.1.14–5.1.15 (miscellaneous).

318 COBS 5.1.2. And see COBS 5.1.3: a firm telephoning a consumer must make its identity and the purpose of its call explicitly clear at the beginning of the conversation.

319 COBS 5.1.16.

320 COBS 5.1.17.

In paragraph 14-071, after "to life policies", replace "in EEA states." with:

14-071   where the state of commitment is the UK.

5. FSMA Imposed Regulatory Liabilities

In the second paragraph, after "(c) liabilities imposed", add:
(or previously imposed) **14-081**

(b) Liabilities Imposed on Authorised Persons

(ii) Liability for Acting Outside Permission

Replace paragraph 14-085 (to incorporate update to text and footnote 388) with:
In general, persons (unless they have the benefit of automatic authorisation) need **14-085** to obtain Part 4A permission in order to undertake any regulated activity.[388] If an authorised person carries on a regulated activity in the UK otherwise than in accordance with his permission, the contravention is actionable in prescribed cases at the suit of a person who suffers consequent loss.[389] Under the relevant prescribing regulations,[390] the right of action is limited to a "private person" as therein defined[391] or a person acting in a fiduciary or representative capacity on behalf of a private person for the latter's benefit. The right of action does not extend to a contravention of a Pt 4A financial resources requirement.

[388] FSMA s.19. As to the grant of Pt 4A permission, see paras 14-012 and 14-013.

[389] FSMA s.20. See *Titan Steel Wheels Ltd v Royal Bank of Scotland Plc* [2010] EWHC 211 (Comm); [2010] 2 Lloyd's Rep. 92 and, under the predecessor provision (1986 Act ss.62 and 62A), *Diamantis Diamantides v JP Morgan Chase Bank* [2005] EWCA Civ 1612 (corporate veil not lifted). See *City Index Ltd (t/a FinSpreads) v Balducci* [2011] EWHC 2562 (Ch); [2012] 1 B.C.L.C. 317: on the facts, no breach of s.20. See also *Camerata Property Inc v Credit Suisse Securities (Europe) Ltd* [2012] EWHC 7 (Comm); [2012] P.N.L.R. 15. See also *Grant Estates Ltd (In Liquidation) v Royal Bank of Scotland* [2012] CSOH 133 at [45]–[62], a Scottish decision of the Outer House, Court of Session.

[390] The FSMA (Rights of Action) Regulations 2001 (SI 2001/2256) regs 4, 3.

[391] See para.14-084.

(c) Liabilities Imposed on EEA Firms

Replace paragraph 14-090 (to incorporate updates to text) with:
The FCA or PRA, as "host state" regulators, were previously empowered to **14-090** impose requirements on "incoming firms".[424] FSMA imposed liability for contravention of such requirements in prescribed cases, at the suit of any person suffering consequent loss.[425] However, FSMA Pt XIII, which previously set out the FCA and PRA's powers in this regard, was largely deleted at the end of the Brexit transition period, by the EEA Passport Rights (Amendment, etc., and Transitional Provisions) (EU Exit) Regulations 2018 (SI 2018/1149). The only provisions in Pt XIII which remain in force are ss.195(3) and (4), preserving the definition of an "overseas regulator" outside of the UK.

[424] See FSMA Pt XIII (ss.193–204).

[425] FSMA s.202. See the Financial Services and Markets Act 2000 (Rights of Action) Regulations 2000 (SI 2000/2256) regs 7, 3.

(d) Liabilities Related to Securities Markets

(ii) Section 90A

FSMA s.90A

Replace paragraph 14-094 (to incorporate update to text and new footnote) with:
Only one claim under s.90A has to date been determined at trial: *ACL* **14-094**

Netherlands BV v Lynch. [448a] As a consequence a number of unresolved questions of law exist. Several of these stem from a mismatch between the language of the statute and the realities of the modern asset management and business environment. In *SL Claimants v Tesco Plc*[449] the court observed that the threshold requirement for bringing a claim (having an "interest in securities") was an "expression derived from a now almost defunct way of doing business", in that it ignored the dematerialised securities market by which investors hold shares in CREST accounts.[450] The court was willing to construe the expression purposively, to include persons with an interest in a trust of such securities.[451] However, questions on this issue remain,[452] and it is submitted that a purposive approach must be taken so as to give the regime teeth, both as a means of compensation and to provide a deterrent to market misstatements.

[448a] [2022] EWHC 1178 (Ch).

[449] [2019] EWHC 2858 (Ch); [2020] Bus. L.R. 250.

[450] *SL Claimants v Tesco Plc* [2019] EWHC 2858 (Ch); [2020] Bus. L.R. 250 at [73].

[451] *SL Claimants v Tesco Plc* [2019] EWHC 2858 (Ch); [2020] Bus. L.R. 250 at [79]–[85].

[452] For example, a common form of European fund structure involves a "management company" which has wide-ranging powers in relation to assets held in a contractually based fund which all investors are a party to (for example, a German law *Sondervermögen* or a French law *fonds commun de placement*). The relevant ownership interests do not fit neatly into English law concepts of legal and beneficial ownership. The management company is the only person with the power to bring a claim on the assets, but it does not "own" them as ultimate beneficial owner. It is to be hoped that the courts would continue with the purposive approach developed in the *Tesco* case.

Replace paragraph 14-095 (to incorporate new text and footnote) with:

14-095   A similar issue arises in relation to the scope of the expression "person discharging managerial responsibility" (or "PDMR") (being the person whose knowledge a claimant must establish). The focus in the statutory wording is on directors of the issuer[453] but limiting it to directors properly so called would appear to permit the regime to be circumvented by listed companies which (as is now common) operate through a board comprising a very small number of executive directors and a larger consultative board of non-executive directors, with the company being operated by non-director executive and management committees comprised of very senior individuals. "PDMR" is a sui generis concept which lends itself to purposive construction in this context. However in *Various Investors v G4S*,[453a] at first instance and in the context of a strike-out application, Miles J rejected the argument that PDMR was an autonomous concept. The Court concluded that a PDMR must be a director. However, that included de facto directors, and there was some potential for "elasticity" in the application of that concept in light of the purposes of s.90A ([180]).

[453] FSMA Sch.10A para.8(5). This includes de facto and shadow directors.

[453a] [2022] EWHC 1081 (Ch); [2022] Bus. L.R. 566.

Replace paragraph 14-096 (to incorporate new text and footnotes) with:

14-096   The meaning of "reliance" is particularly controversial. The reliance must be "on the information in question"[454] which is a reference to the "published information".[455] There is, therefore, no requirement that the "reliance" be on the "untrue or misleading statement" or "omission" (perhaps because the latter is conceptually problematic). A professional asset manager may consider various secondary sources which report on the content of published information such as financial analyst and press reports, or raw data and financial metrics. There is no obvious reason in principle why relying on published information in this manner should be insufficient. Further interesting questions arise where the price determined by the market is itself a function of the information published by the issuer. The Federal Court of Australia has held that acquiring at an inflated price can amount to "market based" or "indirect" causation for the purposes of the equivalent Australian securities statute.[456] In *ACL Netherlands BV v Lynch*,[456a] the court concluded that the focus is on statements or omissions in published information on which reliance is demonstrated to have been placed. It would therefore not be enough to show reliance, in some generalised sense, on a piece of published information, for example the annual report for a given year. The court accepted that an acquirer of shares who relied on part of such an annual report, but did not even look at a misstatement contained elsewhere in that annual report, would not have a cause of action under s.90A. Rather, the person acquiring securities must have applied his mind to the statement in question; and that statement must have induced the acquisition or (on the facts of this particular case) induced the acquirer to transact on the terms he did. That said, the court also concluded that a combination of statements or omissions might create an overall impression which could found a claim.[456b]

[454] FSMA Sch.10A para.3(4)(a).

[455] As referred to in FSMA Sch.10A para.3(1).

[456] *TPT Patrol Pty Ltd v Myer Holdings* [2019] FCA 1747; 140 A.C.S.R. 38.

[456a] [2022] EWHC 1178 (Ch).

[456b] For further analysis of this decision as well as *G4S*, see De Verneuil Smith, Patel and Harman, "UK Securities fraud litigation gains momentum: Autonomy and G4S" [2022] J.I.B.F.L., p.521 (September).

6.   FSMA REMEDIES

(a)   Remedies Available to Regulators

(ii)   Persons against whom Orders Available

Persons knowingly concerned

Replace footnote 486 with:

[486] unreported 26 March 2018 ChD ([2018] 3 WLUK 623). Cited with approval and applied in *Financial Conduct Authority v Avacade Ltd* [2020] EWHC 1673 (Ch) (upheld on appeal: [2021] EWCA Civ 1206). See also *Financial Conduct Authority v Skinner* [2020] EWHC 1097 (Ch); [2020] Lloyd's Rep. F.C. 422, and *Financial Conduct Authority v Ferreira* [2022] EWCA Civ 397; [2022] 1 W.L.R. 2958.   **14-104**

(b)   Remedies Available to Private Litigants

(i)   Recovery of Money or Property Paid under Agreements Made by or Through Unauthorised Person

Contravention of the general prohibition (non-banking)

Replace footnote 525 with:

[525] FSMA ss.26, 26A ("credit-related" activities), 27. As apparent from subs.(3) of each section, it is not retroactive, but note the equivalent provisions in the 1986 Act: ss.5 (relating to investment business) and 132 (relating to insurance contracts). In relation to EEA firms, see FSMA Sch.3, para 16(2): ss.26 and 27 do not apply in relation to agreements entered into by such firms that have not satisfied the conditions for authorisation under those Schedules (but note that these provisions have now been   **14-115**

deleted following the end of the Brexit transition period). For a case under the 1986 Act's provisions, see *CR Sugar Trading Ltd (In Administration) v China National Sugar & Alcohol Group Corp* [2003] EWHC 79 (Comm); [2003] 1 Lloyd's Rep. 279. For a case under s.26, see *Re Whitely Insurance Consultants* [2008] EWHC 1782 (Ch); [2009] Bus. L.R. 418. See also *Andrew Brown v Innovatorone Plc* [2012] EWHC 1321 (Comm) and *Bull v Gain Capital Holdings Inc* [2014] EWHC 539 (Comm).

Contravention of the general prohibition (banking)

Replace footnote 545 with:

14-118   ⁵⁴⁵ FSMA s.29. See Sch.3 para.16(4): disapplication in relation to EEA firms (now deleted following the end of the Brexit transition period).

7.   THE OMBUDSMAN SCHEME

(a)   Introduction

Scope of jurisdictions

Replace paragraph 14-123 (to incorporate update to text and footnote 565) with:

14-123   Under those rules,⁵⁶⁴ the scope of both jurisdictions depends on: (i) the type of activity to which the complaint relates,⁵⁶⁵ (ii) the place where the activity was carried on,⁵⁶⁶ (iii) whether the complainant was "eligible"⁵⁶⁷ and (iv) whether the complaint was referred within the requisite time limit.⁵⁶⁸ The last three conditions are the same for both jurisdictions. As far as the territorial scope of the jurisdictions are concerned, essentially the activity must be carried on from an establishment in the UK.⁵⁶⁹ To be an "eligible claimant" the person must be a "consumer", a "micro-enterprise" (both terms being defined), a small charity or trustee of a small trust fund, a CBTL consumer (in relation to CBTL business), a "small business" or a "guarantor".⁵⁷⁰ The respondent has eight weeks to respond to a complaint by issuing a "final response".⁵⁷¹

⁵⁶⁴ See DISP 2.2.

⁵⁶⁵ DISP 2.3, DISP 2.5, for the two jurisdictions respectively.

⁵⁶⁶ DISP 2.6.

⁵⁶⁷ DISP 2.7.

⁵⁶⁸ DISP 2.8.

⁵⁶⁹ See further, DISP 2.6.

⁵⁷⁰ See further, DISP 2.7 and the *Glossary* for the definition of these terms. A small business may have a turnover of up to £6.5m so long as it employs fewer than 50 persons or has a balance sheet total of less than £5m.

⁵⁷¹ For the "final response", see para.14-128. See further DISP 1.6, 2.8.

(e)   The Investigation

Replace footnote 614 with:

14-133   ⁶¹⁴ For examples of (unsuccessful) challenges to decisions of the Ombudsman see (i) *R. (Norwich & Peterborough Building Society) v Financial Ombudsman Service* [2002] EWHC 2379; [2003] 1 All E.R. (Comm) 65; (ii) *R. (Green Denham) v Financial Ombudsman Service* [2003] EWHC 338 (Admin); (iii) *R. (IFG Financial Services Ltd) v Financial Ombudsman Service* [2005] EWHC 1153 (Admin); [2006] 1 B.C.L.C. 534; (iv) *R. (Heather Moor and Edgecomb Ltd) v Financial Ombudsman Service* [2008] EWCA Civ 643; [2009] 1 All E.R. 328 (fee-charging regime (whereby all firms, even those where complaints were dismissed, had to pay fees to FOS)) was upheld as not irrational; (v) *R. (Keith Williams) v Financial Ombudsman Services* [2008] EWHC 2142 (Admin); (vi) *R. (Bamber & BP Financial Services) v Financial Ombudsman Services* [2009] EWCA Civ 593, and further cases cited below; (vii)

R. (on the application of Green) v Financial Ombudsman Service Ltd [2012] EWHC 1253 (Admin); (viii) *R. (on the application of Bankole) v Financial Ombudsman Service* [2012] EWHC 3555 (Admin); (ix) *R. (on the application of Calland) v Financial Ombudsman Service Ltd* [2013] EWHC 1327 (Admin); (x) *R. (on the application of London Capital Group) v Financial Ombudsman Service Ltd* [2013] EWHC 2425 (Admin); [2014] A.C.D. 3; (xi) *R. (on the application of Fisher) v Financial Ombudsman Service* [2014] EWHC 4928 (Admin); (xii) *Westscott Financial Services Ltd v Financial Ombudsman Service* [2014] EWHC 3972 (Admin); (xiii) *R. (on the application of Chancery (UK) LLP) v Financial Ombudsman Service* [2015] EWHC 407 (Admin); [2015] B.T.C. 13; (xiv) *Full Circle Asset Management Ltd v Financial Ombudsman Service Ltd* [2017] EWHC 323 (Admin); (xv) *R. (on the application of TenetConnect Services Ltd) v Financial Ombudsman* [2018] EWHC 3459 (Admin); [2018] 1 B.C.L.C. 726; [2018] C.T.L.C. 116; (xvi) *R. (on the application of Critchley) v Financial Ombudsman Service Ltd* [2019] EWHC 3036 (Admin); [2020] Lloyd's Rep. I.R. 176; (xvii) *R. (on the application of Portal Financial Services LLP) v Financial Ombudsman Service Ltd* [2022] EWHC 710 (Admin). For successful challenges see: (i) *R. (Garrison Investment Analysis) v Financial Ombudsman Service* [2006] EWHC 2466 (Admin) (decision quashed as being "irrational" in that it was based on an assumption that was unsupported by the evidence); (ii) *R. (British Bankers Association) v Financial Services Authority* [2011] EWHC 999 (Admin); [2011] Bus. L.R. 1531; (iii) *R. (Kelly) v Financial Ombudsman Service Ltd* [2017] EWHC 3581 (Admin); [2018] C.T.L.C. 107; (iv) *R. (on the application of Aviva Life and Pensions (UK) Ltd) v Financial Ombudsman Service* [2017] EWHC 352 (Admin); [2017] Lloyd's Rep. I.R. 404 (FOS determination quashed on basis that it was flawed for inadequacy of reasons); (v) *R. (on the application of Bluefin Insurance Ltd) v Financial Ombudsman Service Ltd* [2014] EWHC 3413 (Admin); [2015] Bus. L.R. 656; [2015] Lloyd's Rep. I.R. 457; (vi) *R. (on the application of TF Global Markets (UK) Ltd (t/a Thinkmarkets)) v Financial Ombudsman Service Ltd* [2020] EWHC 3178 (Admin); [2021] A.C.D. 19. For leave to appeal to challenge FOS, see: *R. (London Capital Group Ltd) v Financial Ombudsman Service Ltd* [2013] EWHC 218 (Admin).

(f) The Award

Money awards.

Replace footnote 629 with:

[629] But not necessarily, see *IFG Financial Services v Financial Ombudsman Service* [2005] EWHC 1153 (Admin); [2006] 1 B.C.L.C. 534 and para.14-132. DISP 3.7.2 (see next note) now explicitly states: "whether or not a court would award compensation". **14-137**

Replace footnote 631 with:

[631] DISP 3.7.4(R). According to this provision, the maximum money award that the Ombudsman may make has now increased to £355,000, if the relevant act or omission took place between 1 April 2020 and 1 April 2022; or £375,000, if the relevant act or omission took place on or after 1 April 2022. **14-138**

Directions

Replace footnote 634 with:

[634] FSMA s.229(1)(b); DISP 3.7.11R. **14-139**

8. FINANCIAL SERVICES COMPENSATION SCHEME

(e) Compensation

(i) Offers of Compensation

Replace paragraph 14-154 (to incorporate updates to text) with:

The FSCS may make reduced or interim offers of compensation if the amount of compensation payable is uncertain or if the claimant has reasonable prospects of recovering part of his loss from any other person.[689] Any offer of compensation made by the FSCS must remain open for 90 days unless it appears during that period that no offer should in fact have been made, or the offer is rejected in that **14-154** period. Upon the expiry of 90 days, the FSCS may withdraw the offer unless its size has been disputed and consideration is being given to making a reduced or interim offer.[690] No offer of compensation will exceed the limits payable by the FSCS for protected claims.[691] For protected investment business (except where the designated investment is a long-term care insurance contract that is a pure protection contract (as defined)), a protected home finance mediation, a protected debt management business or a protected funeral plan business, the limit is now 100% of the claim up to £85,000. For protected investment business (where the designated investment is a long-term care insurance contract that is a pure protection contract (as defined)) or a protected non-investment insurance distribution, the level is again (with certain exceptions) 100% of the claim but there is no maximum payment limit.[692] Customers of firms who have failed and were declared in default prior to 1 April 2019 will still be covered up to the previous £50,000 limits; the new higher limits, however, apply only to claims against firms that fail on or after 1 April 2019.

[689] COMP 8.3.2 and COMP 11.2.4–11.2.6A.

[690] COMP 8.3.1. The offer may also be withdrawn if it is rejected.

[691] See in COMP 10.2. Interest, which may be paid on the compensation sum under COMP 11.2.7, is not to be taken into account when applying limits on the compensation sum payable: COMP 11.2.8.

[692] COMP 10.2.3, Rules 4.1–4.3 of the PRA Depositor Protection Rulebook and Rule 17 of the PRA Policyholder Protection Rulebook.

CHAPTER 15

FINANCIAL PRACTITIONERS

1.   GENERAL

(a) Scope

Replace footnote 2 with:

15-002   ² See Ch.14. The overhaul of the regulatory architecture (see now the Financial Services Act 2012, the Bank of England and Financial Services Act 2016 and the Financial Services Act 2021) did not affect the issues in this chapter (although, most notably, on 1 April 2013, FSMA s.150 was replaced by FSMA s.138D, see para.14-087).

(c) Regulation

In paragraph 15-009, after "is at present", replace "unclear." with:

15-009   unclear, despite the deal reached in December 2020 (as per the UK-EU Trade and Co-operation Agreement and associated declarations) and the end of the Brexit transition period.

2.   DUTIES AND LIABILITIES

(d) The Misrepresentation Act 1967

(i) Relevance

Replace footnote 9 with:

15-014   ⁹ See generally H.G. Beale and others (eds), *Chitty on Contracts*, 34th edn (London: Sweet & Maxwell, 2021), Vol.1, Ch.9. For a successful s.2 claim in the investment context, see *Taberna Europe CDO II Plc v Selskabet (Formerly Roskilde Bank A/S) (In Bankruptcy)* [2015] EWHC 871 (Comm). However on appeal the court held that the bank was entitled to rely upon a disclaimer: [2016] EWCA Civ 1262; [2017] Q.B. 633.

(ii) Representations as to Fact or Opinion: Suitability

Replace paragraph 15-015 (to incorporate updates to footnotes 10 and 11) with:

The traditional view that, to be actionable, a representation must be a statement **15-015**
of fact rather than one of opinion has been considerably eroded in recent years.[10]
It will provide no obstacle to an investor whose complaint is to the effect that an
investment was misdescribed to him. It might appear that a representation as to
"suitability" is more appropriately categorised as a representation of opinion rather
than a representation of fact. Nevertheless, a representor will not escape liability
under the 1967 Act merely because the representation appears to be a statement of
opinion or belief, if the statement carries with it the implication that there are
reasonable grounds for holding that opinion or belief.[11] It is submitted that in many
cases[12] where a financial practitioner recommends an investment as suitable for an
investor, that recommendation carries with it implicit representations that (1) the
nature of the investment has been carefully considered by the practitioner, (2) the
investor's needs have been carefully assessed by the practitioner, and (3) viewed
objectively, the investment meets those needs. If one or more of those implicit
representations is false, the fact that the express representation might be regarded
as one of opinion rather than of fact will be of no assistance to the maker of the
representation.[13]

[10] See generally, *Chitty on Contracts* (2021), Ch.9, paras 9-008 to 9-029. But for findings that statements, in the investment context, were only of "opinion", see *IFE Fund SA v Goldman Sachs
International* [2007] EWCA Civ 811; [2007] 2 Lloyd's Rep. 449; *Springwell Navigation Corp v JP
Morgan Chase Bank* [2010] EWCA Civ 1221; [2010] 2 C.L.C. 705 (considered further at paras 15-037
and 15-053); *Cassa di Risparmio ella Repubblica di San Marino SpA v Barclays Bank Ltd* [2011] EWHC
484 (Comm); [2011] 1 C.L.C. 701.

[11] See *Brown v Raphael* [1958] Ch. 636; *Investors Compensation Scheme Ltd v West Bromwich Building Society* [1999] Lloyd's L. Rep. P.N. 496, noted below.

[12] For examples of statements of "opinion" (which did *not*, on the facts, entail a representation that the
defendant had reasonable grounds for it) see *IFE Fund SA v Goldman Sachs International* [2007] EWCA
Civ 811; [2007] 2 Lloyd's Rep. 449 and *Springwell Navigation Corp v JP Morgan Chase Bank* [2010]
EWCA Civ 1221; [2010] 2 C.L.C. 705 (considered further at paras 15-037 and 15-053).

[13] In *Investors Compensation Scheme Ltd v West Bromwich Building Society* [1999] Lloyd's L. Rep. P.N.
496 the defendant sought to argue that representations to Home Income Plan purchasers ought to be
viewed as nothing more than predictions as to the likely future performance of the Plans and not as
actionable representations. In rejecting this argument Evans-Lombe J considered that, by making the
predictions, the defendant had implicitly stated that it could justify them on reasonable grounds. Since
the defendant could not in fact do so, the representations were prima facie actionable.

(iii) False in a Material Respect

Replace paragraph 15-017 (to incorporate updates to text) with:

No claim will lie under the 1967 Act unless the representation of which complaint **15-017**
is made is false. Difficulty can be encountered if a statement is literally true, but is
nonetheless misleading in certain respects, or if a statement contains elements which
are true and elements which are false. The test often applied has been to ask whether
or not the representation was false in a "material respect".[16] The problem has also
been addressed[17] by applying the test laid down in the (now repealed) s.20(4) of the
Marine Insurance Act 1906; a statement will be treated as being true if it is
substantially correct and the difference would not have induced a reasonable person
to enter the contract.

16 i.e. is the respect in which the representation is false "capable of inducing the representee to enter the contract in question"? See *Lonrho v Al-Fayed (No.2)* [1992] 1 W.L.R. 1.

17 See *Avon Insurance v Swire* [2000] 1 All E.R. (Comm) 573.

(iv) Comparison with Common Law

Replace footnote 20 with:

15-018 20 See *Chitty on Contracts* (2021), Ch.9, para.9-091; *Gran Gelato Ltd v Richcliff (Group) Ltd* [1992] Ch. 560. In the Canadian case of *Avco Financial Services Realty Ltd v Norman* unreported 16 April 2003 the Ontario Court of Appeal concluded that while negligent misrepresentation and contributory negligence could coexist at law, it would be necessary to consider in each case whether the conduct which amounted to reasonable and foreseeable reliance by a claimant on a defendant's representations was nonetheless open to sufficient criticism to justify a finding of contributory negligence on the part of that claimant. *Avco* was cited with approval by the Ontario Supreme Court in *C&B Corrugated Containers Inc v Quadrant Marketing Ltd* [2005] O.T.C 322 (SC); (2005) Can. L.I.I. 14005.

(e) Contractual Duties

(iii) Incorporation of Regulatory Duties in Contract

Replace footnote 31 with:

15-021 31 See generally *Chitty on Contracts* (2021), Ch.16, paras 16-001 to 16-037. See *Marks & Spencer Plc v BNP Paribas Securities Services Trust Co (Jersey) Ltd* [2015] UKSC 72; [2016] A.C. 742.

(iv) Duty of Care and Skill

The duty and the standard

Replace footnote 39 with:

15-022 39 Implied at common law and by reason of the Supply of Goods and Services Act 1982 s.13 (from 1 October 2015 as amended by the Consumer Rights Act 2015 Sch.1 para.38(c)). See also the Consumer Rights Act 2015 s.49. See the interest rate hedging products (IRHPs) misselling cases: *Crestsign Ltd v National Westminster Bank Plc* [2015] EWCA Civ 986; *Hockin v Marsden* [2014] EWHC 763 (Ch); [2014] Bus. L.R. 441; *Kays Hotels Ltd (t/a Claydon Country House Hotel) v Barclays Bank Plc* [2014] EWHC 1927 (Comm). For an example of a situation in which no such implied duty will apply, see *Morley (t/a Morley Estates) v Royal Bank of Scotland Plc* [2021] EWCA Civ 338; [2022] 1 All E.R. (Comm) 703 (permission to appeal to Supreme Court refused).

Replace footnote 49 with:

15-023 49 The claim in respect of a first tranche of investments was held to be the subject of a binding settlement agreement. The claim in respect of a second later tranche of investments also failed: the investments were not unsuitable and the advice given was not negligent.

(v) Agency

Common law agency principles

Replace paragraph 15-027 (to incorporate updates to footnotes 58 and 60) with:

15-027 An agent has implied authority to do whatever is necessary for, or ordinarily incidental to, the effective execution of his express authority in the usual way.[58] This has two consequences. First, while the terms of an appointed representative's express authority might be limited to providing investment advice to customers in relation to particular products of his principal, conduct that is incidental to the provision of that advice (such as soliciting the customers, identifying the financial and personal circumstances of the particular customer, assisting in any application that the customer might choose to make) will still fall within the actual authority of that representative. Hence in *Martin v Britannia Life Ltd*,[59] the representative was authorised only to give advice in relation to "investments" issued by the defendant. However, he also gave mortgage advice (a mortgage of real property (then) not being an "investment"). It was held that he had actual authority to give such advice since the advice was inherently bound up with and incidental to the advice given by him in relation to the other investments. Secondly, irrespective of whether or not the agent has actual authority to act on the principal's behalf in the relevant way, a principal will be bound by such acts of an agent if the agent has ostensible or apparent authority to act in that way.[60] Thus, if a firm has knowingly or even unwittingly led a customer to believe that an appointed representative or other agent is authorised to conduct business on its behalf of a type that he is not in fact authorised to conduct, the firm will be bound by the acts and omissions of the agent and will be liable for his defaults.[61]

[58] See P.G. Watts and F.M.B. Reynolds (eds), *Bowstead & Reynolds on Agency*, 22nd edn (London: Sweet & Maxwell, 2021, 1st supp, 2021), art.27 at paras 3-022 onwards.

[59] [2000] Lloyd's L. Rep. P.N. 412 at [426]–[428] per Jonathan Parker J (on the predecessor to the FSMA s.39); considered also at para.15-059. However, the claim failed as it was statute-barred.

[60] See generally as to ostensible authority, *Freeman & Lockyer v Buckhurst Park Properties (Mangal) Ltd* [1964] 2 Q.B. 480 at [503] per Diplock LJ and *Bowstead & Reynolds on Agency* (2021, 1st supp, 2021), art.27 at paras 3-004 onwards.

[61] In *Martin v Britannia Life Ltd* [2000] Lloyd's Rep. P.N. 412, the representative gave a business card (with which he had been supplied by the defendant) to the customer which bore the defendant's name and logo, the representative's name and the words "Financial Adviser". Jonathan Parker J held that this was sufficient on the facts of the case to provide the representative with ostensible authority to advise in a far wider capacity than that in which the defendant had expressly authorised him to advise. The defendant was therefore liable for the representative's conduct.

(f)   Tort-based Duties

(i)   Deceit or Fraudulent Misrepresentation

General

Replace footnote 62 with:

[62] See generally M.A. Jones, A. Dugdale and others (eds), *Clerk & Lindsell on Torts*, 23rd edn (London: Sweet & Maxwell, 2020, 2nd supp, 2022), Ch.17, paras 17-01 onwards.

15-028

Replace paragraph 15-034 (to incorporate new text and footnote) with:

Benchmark manipulation litigation has given rise to a number of important cases on deceit in respect of financial products. In *Property Alliance Group Ltd v Royal Bank of Scotland*[73] the Court of Appeal accepted that a bank's conduct in proposing a swap based on LIBOR carried an implied representation that the bank was not itself seeking to manipulate LIBOR, though the claim failed for other reasons. In *Leeds City Council v Barclays Bank Plc*[74] the question was whether the claimant needed to have a conscious awareness of the state of affairs being represented, or whether it was enough (as the claimants contended) to assume that the benchmark was not being manipulated by the defendant. On a summary judgment application Cockerill J found for the defendants and dismissed the claims. The decision is controversial since the assumption was itself arguably induced by the

15-034

misrepresentation. Its wider consequences remain to be seen. It was not followed on this point by Waksman J *Crossley v Volkswagen Group*.[74a]

[73] [2018] EWCA Civ 355; [2018] 1 W.L.R. 3529.

[74] [2021] EWHC 363 (Comm); [2021] 3 W.L.R. 1180.

[74a] [2021] EWHC 3444 (QB).

(iii)   Negligence

Clients

Replace footnote 85 with:

15-038   [85] [2011] EWHC 2304 (QB); [2011] 2 C.L.C. 459; [2012] P.N.L.R. 7 at [70]. After referring to the decisions in *JP Morgan Chase Bank v Springwell Navigation Corp* [2008] EWHC 1186 (Comm), *Wilson v MF Global UK Ltd* [2011] EWHC 138 (QB) and *Bank Leumi (UK) Plc v Wachner* [2011] EWHC 656 (Comm); [2011] 1 C.L.C. 454, the judge stated:

> "But the relationships between adviser and client in those cases were factually very different. They were all experienced investors who conducted transactions through their investment managers over a substantial period of time on an execution only basis, and who from time to time had received expressions of opinion about categories of investment which, in isolation, could be construed as advice. The present case concerns a one-to-one inquiry about a specific investment transaction. If advice was given by Mr Marsden, which led to a transaction being concluded on the basis of that advice, I see no obstacle, in terms of proximity or assumption of responsibility in the *Hedley Byrne /Henderson v Merrett* sense, why a duty of care would not have been owed at the time the advice was given, or why subsequently the advice should not have acquired contractual force when the contract was entered into."

See also *Grant Estates Ltd (In Liquidation) v Royal Bank of Scotland* [2012] CSOH 133. The judge, Lord Hodge, derived five propositions from the English authorities as to the issue whether a duty of care arose in an investment advisory context. See also *Perks v Royal Bank of Scotland* [2022] EWHC 726 (Comm) which contains a detailed exposition of the indicia of an advisory relationship in a swaps misselling context at [271].

Third parties

After the first paragraph, add new paragraph:

15-041   In *Royal Bank of Scotland International Ltd v JP SPC 4*[90a] the Privy Council rejected an investment fund's argument that the bank owed the fund a tortious duty of care, in circumstances where the fund was said to be the beneficial owner of funds held in two of the bank's accounts which had allegedly been fraudulently misappropriated by the bank's customer. The Board found that such a duty did not exist on the basis of the *Quincecare* duty of care, as set out in *Barclays Bank Plc v Quincecare Ltd*[90b] and subsequently applied in (amongst other cases) *Philipp v Barclays Bank Plc*,[90c] and that the recognition of such a duty would not constitute an appropriate incremental development of existing authorities on duties of care to protect third parties from economic loss.

[90a] [2022] UKPC 18; [2022] 3 W.L.R. 261.

[90b] [1992] 4 All E.R. 363.

[90c] [2022] EWCA Civ 318; [2022] Q.B. 578.

3.   BREACH OF DUTY

(b)   Misleading Promotion

(i)   Old Prospectus Cases

Replace footnote 133 with:

[133] See *Aaron's Reefs v Twiss* [1896] A.C. 273. See also in the context of periodic financial reporting, *ACL Netherlands v Lynch* [2022] EWHC 1178 (Ch); an action can lie if statements or omissions work in combination to create an overall impression which is rendered false ([506]). See further the FCA's Decision Notice dated 24 June 2022 in respect of Carillion Plc and its directors, finding general, positive statements to have been "misleading".

15-055

(iv)   Advising and Selling

After the first paragraph, add new paragraph:

In order to decide whether to recommend a product an advisor must gain a sufficient understanding of it. In *Page v Financial Conduct Authority*[159a] the Upper Tribunal found that it was not open to an advisor to rely on the inadequacy of its own resources to contend that it should be given more latitude in respect of product due diligence. If an adviser was unable to obtain an adequate understanding of the product, it should not be recommended at all ([292]–[294]). A greater level of due diligence and care is needed in respect of unregulated products as compared with regulated ones ([295]).

15-062

[159a] [2022] UKUT 124 (TCC).

Replace paragraph 15-063 (to incorporate updates to footnotes) with:

An anterior issue is whether an advisory duty is owed at all. In *Adams v Options UK Personal Pensions LLP*[160] the Court of Appeal endorsed earlier High Court authority to the effect that the giving of mere information may constitute advice where the provision of information is itself the product of a selection process involving a value judgment such that it would tend to influence the decision of the recipient. An element of comparison or evaluation is also likely to cross the dividing line from information to advice, as is a communication to the effect that the recipient ought to invest.[161] Further, while advice to invest in a particular class of assets would not constitute advice on investments for the purposes of art.53 of the Regulated Activities Order, more specific advice would do, notwithstanding that the investment recommended might have permutations (such as a different class of shares). Of course the former type of recommendation may nevertheless give rise to a claim in negligence or breach of COBS rules.

15-063

[160] [2021] EWCA Civ 474; [2021] Bus. L.R. 1568. The decision resolves a number of important points relating to liability for supposed "execution only" pension transfers. See also *Berkeley Burke SIPP Administrators Ltd v Financial Ombudsman Service Ltd* [2018] EWHC 2878 (Admin); [2019] Bus. L.R. 437.

[161] [2021] EWCA Civ 474; [2021] Bus. L.R. 1568 at [75]. See also *Perks v Royal Bank of Scotland* [2022] EWHC 726 (Comm) (bank found to have given a "steer" to client engaging COBS 9, at [404]).

4.   DEFENCES AND RELIEF

(c)   Restriction of Liability by Contract

Unfair Contract Terms Act 1977

Replace footnote 185 with:

15-076   [185] See further paras 2-037, 2-056, 2-059 and 5-015 onwards. The Consumer Rights Act 2015 Pt 2 rationalises the law on unfair terms in consumer contracts. It amends UCTA so as confine it to non-consumers (with "consumers", as defined, being covered by the Consumer Rights Act 2015).

Consumer Rights Act 2015 Pt 2

Replace footnote 207 with:

15-078   [207] See further *Chitty on Contracts* (2021), Ch.40.

5.   REMEDIES INCLUDING DAMAGES

(b)   Damages: Causation, Duty Nexus and Legal Responsibility for Loss

(i)   Causation

Replace footnote 224 with:

15-087   [224] [2004] UKHL 41; [2005] 1 A.C. 134. See para.13-089.

CHAPTER 16

INSURANCE BROKERS

2.   LIABILITY FOR BREACH OF DUTY

(d)   Failing to Effect Insurance Which Meets the Client's Requirements

Where the client becomes involved in a dispute with the insurer

Replace footnote 184 with:

16-067   184 For a further illustration, see *Ramco Ltd v Weller Russell & Laws Insurance Brokers Ltd* [2008] EWHC 2202 (QB); [2009] Lloyd's Rep. I.R. 27; [2009] P.N.L.R. 14 in which David Donaldson QC, sitting as a Deputy High Court Judge, held that the broker was in breach of its obligation to obtain insurance which clearly and indisputably met its client's requirements owing to the existence of wording in the policy which introduced complications and was possibly fatal to the insured's entitlement to an indemnity from the insurer. In *Synergy Health (UK) Ltd v CGU Insurance Plc* [2010] EWHC 2583 (Comm); [2011] Lloyd's Rep. I.R. 500, Flaux J held that the broker's duty was:

> "to take reasonable care to obtain insurance that clearly met [the client's] requirements and did not involve unnecessary risks of litigation about its legal scope and effect."

In *ABN AMRO Bank NV v Royal and Sun Alliance Insurance Plc* [2021] EWHC 442 (Comm) Jacobs J held that a broker was in breach of its obligation to obtain insurance which: (i) clearly and indisputably met the client's requirements; and (ii) did not expose the client to an unnecessary risk of litigation. The broker was in breach of duty because the broker had failed to check that the insurer had the same understanding as the insured regarding the existence of credit risk cover afforded by an unusual clause in a policy of cargo insurance. The judge held that the broker was in breach of duty even on the premise that the policy did afford the cover sought by the insured (at [935]). This issue was not addressed on appeal, in which it was held that the insured had full cover for its loss: [2021] EWCA Civ 1789; [2022] 1 W.L.R. 1773.

Inadequate level of cover

Replace footnote 194 with:

16-070   194 [1999] Lloyd's Rep. P.N. 598, Moore-Bick J. See also *Kennedy (BJ) Agency (1984) Ltd v Kilgour Bell Ins* (1999) 139 Man. R. (2d) 276, Manitoba QB, in which the broker was negligent in failing to advise his client of the availability of "replacement cost coverage" and the limitations of "actual value" coverage. See also *Cafe de Lecq Ltd v R.A. Rossborough (Insurance Brokers) Ltd* [2012] JRC053 (Royal Court of Jersey) in which the broker was found to be in breach of duty in failing to advise his client that the sum insured for buildings' cover should represent the cost of reinstating the buildings in the event of their destruction.

(j)   Failing to Give Proper Advice

Seeking the insurer's advice

Replace footnote 309 with:

16-120   309 In *Dodson v Dodson Insurance Services* [2001] 1 W.L.R. 1012, the Court of Appeal suggested (at [21]) that, if there was some uncertainty about the scope of cover afforded by a policy, then the broker should not give advice in unqualified terms or without first confirming the scope of cover with the insurer. In *ABN Amro Bank NV v Royal and Sun Alliance Insurance Plc* [2021] EWHC 442 (Comm) Jacobs J. held that the broker was in breach of duty in failing to discuss with the insurer the effect of an unusual credit risk clause in a cargo policy, to ensure that there was no misunderstanding or uncertainty as to the scope of cover afforded by that clause. This issue was not addressed in the subsequent appeal in which it was held that the insured had full cover for its loss: [2021] EWCA Civ 1789; [2022] 1 W.L.R. 1773.

3. Damages

(a) Factual Causation

Would the insured loss have occurred?

Replace footnote 372 with:

372 *Mint Security Ltd v Blair* [1982] 1 Lloyd's Rep. 188; *O&R Jewellers Ltd v Terry* [1999] Lloyd's Rep. **16-148**
I.R. 463 and *Cee Bee Marine Ltd v Lombard Insurance Co Ltd* [1990] 2 N.Z.L.R. 1 (see para.16-140).
The decision in *Nicholas G Jones v Environcom Ltd* was distinguished by HHJ Waksman QC (sitting
as Judge of the High Court) in *RR Securities Ltd v Towergate Underwriting Group Ltd* [2016] EWHC
2653 at [57]–[68]. In *ABN AMRO Bank NV v RSA* [2021] EWHC 442 (Comm) Jacobs J. held that damages were recoverable by the insured on the basis that, if the broker had acted with due skill and care,
then either (i) credit risk cover would have been arranged, or if such cover had been unavailable, then
(ii) the insured would have unwound the transactions which ultimately gave rise to its loss. This issue
was not addressed in the subsequent appeal in which it was held that the insured had full cover for its
loss: [2021] EWCA Civ 1789; [2022] 1 W.L.R. 1773.

(c) Legal Responsibility

(ii) Foreseeability

Replace footnote 407 with:

407 See *Nicholas G Jones v Environcom Ltd* [2010] EWHC 759 (Comm); [2010] Lloyd's Rep. I.R. 676; **16-166**
[2010] P.N.L.R. 27, Steel J (discussed at para.16-148). In *ABN AMRO Bank NV v RSA* [2021] EWHC
442 (Comm) Jacobs J. held that the claimant bank was entitled to recover damages on the basis that, if
the broker had acted with due skill and care, then either (i) it would have obtained credit risk cover in
relation to certain transactions or, if such cover had been unavailable, then (ii) the insured would have
unwound the transactions which ultimately gave rise to the loss. This issue was not addressed in the
subsequent appeal in which it was held that the insured had full cover for its loss: [2021] EWCA Civ
1789; [2022] 1 W.L.R. 1773.

(d) The Measure of Damages

Litigation costs

Replace footnote 452 with:

452 [2021] EWHC 442 (Comm) at [1036], Jacobs J. This issue was not addressed in the subsequent **16-184**
appeal: [2021] EWCA Civ 1789; [2022] 1 W.L.R. 1773.

Credit for saved premium

Replace footnote 463 with:

463 [2006] EWHC 424; [2006] 1 All E.R. (Comm) 789 at [317]. Similarly in *Pakeezah Meat Supplies* **16-186**
Ltd v Total Insurance Solutions Ltd [2018] EWHC 1141 (Comm); [2019] Lloyd's Rep. I.R. 137 Butcher
J held (at [23]) that an assessment of the client's loss had to take into account the additional premium
that would have been payable by the client. Again in *ABN AMRO Bank NV v RSA* [2021] EWHC 442
(Comm) Jacobs J held (at [1020]) that an assessment of the insured's loss required credit to be given
for saved premium. This issue was not addressed in the subsequent appeal: [2021] EWCA Civ 1789;
[2022] 1 W.L.R. 1773.

ACCOUNTANTS AND AUDITORS

2. DUTIES

(d) The Standard of Skill and Care

(ii) Auditing

Auditing standards

Replace footnote 268 with:

17-090   [268] The current ISAs (which are effective for audits of financial statements for periods commencing on or after 17 June 2016) and other documents referred to in this section are available on the FRC website. The previous standards, known as Statements of Auditing Standards (SASs), and historic versions of the ISAs are also available on that website. In this chapter the references are primarily to the ISAs. ISA 250 and ISA 330 were revised in 2017, and those revisions required other ISAs to be updated: ISQC 1, ISA 210, ISA 220, ISA 240, ISA 260, ISA 450, ISA 500 and ISA 505. Those revisions and updates are effective for periods commencing on or after 15 December 2017. Further revisions and updates were made in 2019 and 2020 in respect of the Glossary of Terms, ISQC1, and ISAs 200, 220, 230, 240, 250, 260, 315, 500, 570, 580, 600, 620, 700, 701 and 720. They are effective for engagements relating to financial periods commencing on or after 15 December 2019 and those revisions required other ISAs to be updated: ISQC 1, ISA 210, ISA 220, ISA 240, ISA 260, ISA 450, ISA 500 and ISA 505. Further revisions and updates were made in 2021. ISQC 1 has been replaced by ISQM 1, and ISQM 2 has been introduced. The former deals with the firm's responsibility to establish policies or procedures addressing engagements that are required to be subject to engagement quality reviews. The latter deals with the appointment and eligibility of the engagement quality reviewer, and the performance and documentation of the engagement quality review. They will each be effective as of 15 December 2022. ISA 220 and 240 have also been revised in July and May 2021 respectively. Those revisions will be effective for periods on or after 15 December 2021. The majority of the ISAs and ISQC1 were updated in May 2022, which incorporate conforming amendments made as a result of the revision of ISA (UK) 315 (Revised July 2020). These amendments become effective for audits of financial statements for periods beginning on or after 15 December 2021.

CHAPTER 18

ACTUARIES

2. DUTIES

(a) The Statutory Context

(i) Pensions

Occupational pension schemes

Replace footnote 6 with:

[6] For a detailed consideration of occupational pension schemes, the reader is referred to R. Ellison (ed.),   **18-007**
Pensions Law and Practice, Rel.69 (London: Sweet & Maxwell, 2022).

(b) Duties to Client

(i) Contractual Duties

Replace paragraph 18-020 with:

In theory it is possible that third parties may be identified in the actuary's contract   **18-020**
and hence fall within the Contracts (Rights of Third Parties) Act 1999. In practice, as with other areas of professional negligence, the Act has so far been of little practical significance.

CHAPTER 20

INFORMATION TECHNOLOGY PROFESSIONALS

1. GENERAL

Replace footnote 1 with:

20-001 ¹ Much of the chapter concerns the supply of software, which may be the subject of copyright and/or duties of confidentiality. Liability arising from breaches of copyright and/or confidence is, however, beyond the scope of this book, and the reader should consult specialist works in this area: C. Phipps, S. Teasdale and W. Harman (eds), *Toulson & Phipps on Confidentiality*, 4th edn (London: Sweet & Maxwell, 2020) and G. Harbottle, N. Caddick and U. Suthersanen (eds), *Copinger and Skone James on Copyright*, 18th edn (London: Sweet & Maxwell, 2021, 1st supp, 2022).

2. DUTIES

(a) Duties to Client

(ii) Contracts for Services

Replace footnote 7 with:

20-005 ⁷ See para.20-012.

(iv) Bespoke Software

Replace footnote 13 with:

20-012 ¹³ A survey of the case law is contained in the decision of the Court of Appeal in *Computer Associates UK Ltd v Software Incubator Ltd* [2018] EWCA Civ 518; [2018] 2 All E.R. (Comm) 398. See also M. Bridge and others (eds), *Benjamin's Sale of Goods*, 11th edn (London: Sweet & Maxwell, 2021, 1st supp, 2022), Ch.1, para.1-080.

Replace footnote 21 with:

20-014 ²¹ See *Benjamin's Sale of Goods* (2021, 1st supp, 2022), Ch.1, para.1-086; *Gretton & Starkey (t/a Open Systems Design) v British Millerain Co Ltd* unreported 29 July 1998, HH Judge Thornton QC.

Replace paragraph 20-016 (to incorporate new text and footnote) with:

20-016 The case of *St Albans City and DC v International Computers Ltd* was considered by the Court of Appeal in *Computer Associates UK Ltd v Software Incubator Ltd.*²⁴ The case concerned the correct interpretation of reg.17 of the Commercial Agents (Council Directive) Regulations 1993, and whether for the purposes of the Regulations "goods" could include software which had been supplied electronically. Reversing the decision at first instance on this issue, the Court of Appeal held that such software did not constitute "goods" within the meaning of the Regulations. In reaching that decision, giving the leading judgment, Gloster LJ surveyed relevant domestic, Commonwealth, and EU case law, and considered a number of leading academic texts. Gloster LJ noted that it was difficult, as a matter of principle, to see why software should be treated differently depending on the mode of its delivery. She also expressed "sympathy" with the view that the failure to treat software and other intangibles as goods put the law out of step with recent technological developments and seemed artificial in the modern age. However, the Court considered itself bound by precedent to interpret the Regulations to exclude software. In doing so, the Court stated that an approach which departed from precedent and the well understood meaning of "goods" in law should be resisted by the judiciary.[25] However, in response to a request from the Supreme Court for a preliminary ruling on the issue the European Union Court of Justice held that the expression "sale of goods" in art.1(2) of the Commercial Agents Directive (86/653/EEC) (Directive) covers the supply, in return for a fee, of computer software to a customer by electronic means where that supply is accompanied by the grant of a perpetual user licence. [25a]

[24] [2018] EWCA Civ 518; [2018] 2 All E.R. (Comm) 398.

[25] [2018] EWCA Civ 518; [2018] 2 All E.R. (Comm) 398 at [45]

[25a] The *Software Incubator Ltd v Computer Associates* (UK) Ltd (C-410/19) EU:C:2021:742; [2022] 2 All E.R. (Comm) 139 (16 September 2021).

5.   REMEDIES

(d)   **Restitution**

Replace footnote 155 with:

[155] See C. Mitchell, and S. Wattterson (eds), Goff & Jones, *The Law of Unjust Enrichment*, 9th edn   **20-106** (London: Sweet & Maxwell, 2016) (10th edn, forthcoming, 2022).

6.   EXCLUSION AND LIMITATION OF LIABILITY

Replace footnote 159 with:

[159] As to such clauses, see paras 5-001 to 5-035, including paras 5-027 to 5-031 as to the Consumer   **20-109** Rights Act 2015. See H.G. Beale and others (eds), *Chitty on Contracts*, 34th edn (London: Sweet & Maxwell 2021), for a comprehensive coverage of this area of law.

7.   MITIGATION

Replace footnote 174 with:

[174] See, e.g. J. Edelman and others (eds), *McGregor on Damages*, 21st edn (London: Sweet & Maxwell,   **20-122** 2021, 1st supp, 2021), Ch.9, paras 9-014 onwards.

CHAPTER 21

PATENT ATTORNEYS AND TRADE MARK ATTORNEYS

1. GENERAL

(a) The Function of a Patent Attorney

21-002

Replace heading footnote 5 with: For a general exposition of the law relating to patents, see Sir Colin Birss, D. Campbell and others (eds), *Terrell on the Law of Patents*, 19th edn (London: Sweet & Maxwell, 2020, 1st supp, 2021). For the statutory framework relating to patent attorneys, see Lord MacKay of Clashfern and others (eds), *Halsbury's Laws of England*, 5th edn (London: LexisNexis, 2020, cum supp pt 2, Vol.50–104, 2022), Vol.79 (reissue), paras 614–651.

(b) The Function of a Trade Mark Attorney

Replace footnote 22 with:

21-006

22 For the law relating to trademarks, see J. Mellor and others (eds), *Kerly's Law of Trade Marks and Tradenames*, 16th edn (London: Sweet & Maxwell, 2017, 1st supp, 2021).

(c) Duties to Clients

After paragraph 21-010, add new paragraph:

21-010A

There are no special rules in patent cases for determining precisely which parties were in fact the patent attorney's client(s), or to whom tortious duties of care were owed—the court will apply the same analytical framework as in cases involving other professionals. An example of this analytical framework being applied can be seen in the recent patent attorney case of *BASF Corp v Carpmaels and Ransford*

(A Firm).[33a] In that case four companies within the BASF group contended that they were the clients of the patent attorney defendant and/or that tortious duties of care were owed to each company. Adam Johnson J rejected the contentions of the second to fourth claimants, conducting a careful analysis and application of the law of express and implied retainers (at [296]—[310]) and assumption of responsibility (at [311]—[321]).

[33a] [2021] EWHC 2899 (Ch).

2. LIABILITY FOR BREACH OF DUTY

General

Replace paragraph 21-017 (to incorporate new text and footnote) with:

21-017   Given the paucity of reported cases, there are few illustrations of the type of circumstances in which patent attorneys or trade mark attorneys may be found to be negligent. One particular area in which patent attorneys and trade mark attorneys are obviously vulnerable is in relation to missing deadlines for the registration of documents. An illustration is afforded by *Kerr v Laurence Shaw & Associates.*[47] In that case the claimant asked patent agents to delay a patent application in North America until the last moment, which was over a year away, but they failed to do so. Proudman J held that the defendants were negligent in failing to implement a system of reminders or remind the claimant of the deadline. In *BASF Corp v Carpmaels and Ransford (A Firm)*[47a] the defendant patent attorneys admitted negligence in respect of failing to lodge an appeal in time to the Technical Board of Appeal from a decision of the European Patent Office's Opposition Division, revoking the patent in question for lack of inventive step.

[47] [2010] EWHC 585 (Ch); [2010] P.N.L.R. 24.

[47a] [2021] EWHC 2899 (Ch).

3. DAMAGES

Causation and loss of a chance

Replace paragraph 21-025 (to incorporate new text and footnote) with:

21-025   Consonant with the general law,[68] a claimant will have to prove on the balance of probabilities that he would have acted differently if properly advised, for instance in prosecuting a patent application. This is a question of causation. If this hurdle is overcome, quantification of damages takes place on a less onerous basis: the claimant will recover damages if there was a significant (i.e. non-negligible) chance that it would have been financially better off if that course of action had been pursued (for example, that it would have obtained a valuable patent). This may involve considering whether the patent would have been granted, whether revocation proceedings might have been brought[69] and what the results of those proceedings would have been, and whether a competitor could easily have avoided infringing such claims.[70] In *Kerr v Lawrence Shaw & Associates,*[71] the court held that the claimant suffered no loss, because on the balance of probabilities he would not have applied for a Canadian patent if reminded to do so, the patent would have been invalid due to prior art unless amended (as was conceded, so the issue was not a matter of the loss of a chance), and on the balance of probabilities the claimant would not have made the necessary amendments. In *Baillie v Bromhead & Co,*[72] the court held that although the defendant patent attorney had given inexplicable and negligent advice the loss suffered by the claimants had not been caused by that advice. In *BASF Corp v Carpmaels and Ransford (A Firm)*[72a] the court carried out a detailed analysis of the types of losses which were claimed, the precise basis upon which they were claimed, and whether there was a real and substantial chance that the defendant's admitted breach of duty had caused loss and damage as alleged. In a passage which is useful in including a summary of the relevant "loss of a chance" jurisprudence (at [322]–[344]), Adam Johnson J concluded (at [355]) that the claimants could not demonstrate that the existence of the patent would have led to more favourable procurement decisions being made by OEMs, or that there would have been an opportunity to negotiate an increased royalty rate, or that any such negotiations would have led to a higher royalty rate. The claim for substantial damages accordingly failed.

[68] See *Allied Maples v Simmons & Simmons* [1995] 1 W.L.R. 1602.

[69] Pursuant to the Patents Act 1977 s.72. Compare *Alexander Turnbull & Co Ltd v Cruickshank and Fairweather* (1905) 22 R.P.C. 521, where the Inner House of the Court of Session struck out a plea in a patent agent's negligence case that the patent was invalid for want of novelty, a decision which would probably not be followed now.

[70] Some indication of the factors that may have to be taken into account are given by Buckley LJ in *Andrew Master Hones Ltd v Cruikshank and Fairweather* [1981] R.P.C. 389 at 403, ll.29–38.

[71] [2010] EWHC 585 (Ch); [2010] P.N.L.R. 24.

[72] [2014] EWHC 2149 (Ch); [2015] F.S.R. 16 at [333].

[72a] [2021] EWHC 2899 (Ch).

CHAPTER 22

ART PROFESSIONALS

1.   GENERAL

Professional regulation

Replace footnote 2 with:

[2] See *https://www.propertymark.co.uk/professional-standards/rules.html* [Accessed 29 September 2022]. **22-007**

(a)   Duties to Client

(i)   *Contractual Duties*

Replace footnote 11 with:

[11] For which purpose see M. Bridge and others (eds), *Benjamin's Sale of Goods*, 11th edn (London: **22-009** Sweet & Maxwell, 2021, 1st supp, 2022).

Replace footnote 14 with:

[14] For illustration see *Harlingdon Enterprises v C Hull Fine Art Ltd* [1991] 1 Q.B. 564 (sale of two paint- **22-011** ings attributed to Gabriele Munter not a sale by description) and *Mansour Ojjeh v Marke Waller* [1998]

12 WLUK 288 (sale of glass mascots attributed to Lalique was a sale by description). In *Drake v Thos Agnew & Sons Ltd* [2002] EWHC 294 (QB); Telegraph 21 March 2002, Buckley J summarised the applicable law before finding that it was not a condition of a sale by a gallery that a particular painting be by van Dyck.

(b)   Duties to Third Parties

Replace footnote 25 with:

22-014   [25] Which the Supreme Court described as the foundation of liability in tort for negligent misrepresentation in *Steel v NRAM Ltd* [2018] UKSC 13; [2018] 1 W.L.R. 1190. See paras 2-096 to 2-110.

Charlesworth & Percy on Negligence, 15th Edition

General Editor: *Mark Armitage*

ISBN: 9780414102903

June 2022

Hardback/ProView eBook/Westlaw UK

As the foremost guide ***Charlesworth & Percy on Negligence*** offers unrivalled depth of analysis into the tort of negligence. Building on the excellence of previous editions, the 15th edition focuses on the considerable body of new case law that has emerged since the previous edition and recent legislative changes.

The new edition discusses the following key case law to name a few:

In the Supreme Court

- *Manchester Building Society v Grant Thornton UK LLP* [2021] UKSC 20 – examining the fundamental ingredients of the modern tort of negligence and the significance of the scope of a defendant's duty of care in relation to issues of both duty and causation.
- *Khan v Meadows* [2021] UKSC 21 – consideration of the principles developed in *Manchester Building Society* in the context of a claim for clinical negligence.

In the Court of Appeal

- *Ford v Seymour-Williams* [2021] EWCA Civ 1848 – examining the ingredients required for a finding of liability pursuant to s.2(2) Animals Act 1980.
- *Blackpool Football Club Ltd v DSN* [2021] EWCA Civ 1352 – application of the principles of vicarious liability in relation to the actions of an unpaid football scout.

Clerk & Lindsell on Torts, 2nd Supplement to the 23rd Edition

General Editor: *Andrew Tettenborn*

ISBN: 9780414103474

June 2022

Paperback/ProView eBook/Westlaw UK

Clerk & Lindsell on Torts, one of our flagship titles and part of the Common Law Library series, is an essential reference tool which is widely referred to by practitioners and cited by the judiciary. It offers the most comprehensive coverage of the subject, providing the end user with indispensable access to current, frequent and unrivalled authoritative information on all aspects of tort law.

The new supplement brings the Main Work fully up to date with the latest developments (including, where appropriate, the fallout from the completion of the Brexit process). These include, among others:

• *ZXC v Bloomberg* on misuse of private information and breach of copyright.

• *Secretary of State for Health v Servier Laboratories Ltd* on the economic torts and unlawful means.

• *McQuillan's Application for Judicial Review* on timing and liability under the Human Rights Act 1998.

• *Bell v Tavistock & Portman NHS Foundation Trust* on young persons and consent to gender reassignment.

• *Barking & Dagenham LBC v Persons Unknown* on property, injunctions, and anonymous trespassers.

Asbestos: Law & Litigation, 2nd Edition

General Editors: *Harry Steinberg QC, Michael Rawlinson QC and James Beeton*

ISBN: 9780414102330

June 2022

Hardback/ProView eBook/Westlaw UK

Asbestos: Law & Litigation is the first comprehensive guide to claims for asbestos-related injury in the UK. It has been written by experienced practitioners involved in many of the leading cases on the subject. The scope of the book is wide-ranging; from the development of knowledge, to the law of damages, with all of the legal and practical issues in between.

The new edition discusses the following key case law to name a few:

Steve Hill Ltd v Witham, Head v Culver Heating Co Ltd and *Rix v Paramount Shopfitting Company Ltd*: a recent trilogy of Court of Appeal judgments which clarified the proper approach to the assessment of losses in asbestos disease claims.

Bussey v Anglia Heating Ltd: a key Court of Appeal decision concerning the correct approach to foreseeable risks in tort law and the impact and relevance of important technical guidance documents in asbestos claims.

HMG3 LTD v Dunn: bespoke High Court guidance on the court's approach to the exercise of its discretion to disapply the primary limitation period in cases involving claims for fatal asbestos disease.

Contact us on :   Tel: +44 (0)345 600 9355

Order online: sweetandmaxwell.co.uk